THE Vegetarian COLLECTION

TRANSCONTINENTAL BOOKS

1100 René-Lévesque Boulevard West
24th floor
Montreal, Que. H3B 4X9
Tel: (514) 340-3587
Toll-free: 1-866-800-2500
www.canadianliving.com

Bibliothèque et Archives nationales du Québec
and Library and Archives Canada cataloguing
in publication

Kent, Alison
The vegetarian collection: creative meat-free dishes
that nourish & inspire
"Canadian living".
Includes index.
ISBN 978-0-9813938-0-3
1. Vegetarian cookery. I. Canadian living. II. Title.

TX837.K462 2010   641.5´636   C2010-941083-1

Project editor: Christina Anson Mine
Copy editor: Austen Gilliland
Indexer: Gillian Watts
Creative direction: Michael Erb
Art direction and design: Chris Bond
Production coordinator: Erin Poetschke

Printed in Canada
© Transcontinental Books, 2010
Legal deposit – 3rd quarter 2010
National Library of Quebec
National Library of Canada
ISBN 978-0-9813938-0-3

We acknowledge the financial support of
our publishing activity by the Government
of Canada through the BPDIP program of the
Department of Canadian Heritage.

For information on special rates for
corporate libraries and wholesale purchases,
please call 1-866-800-2500.

Canadian Living

THE Vegetarian COLLECTION

CREATIVE MEAT-FREE DISHES THAT NOURISH & INSPIRE

By Alison Kent & The Canadian Living Test Kitchen

Transcontinental Books

[EDITOR'S NOTE

MEATLESS DISHES THAT SPUR – NOT SQUASH – CREATIVITY

Think "delicious and satisfying vegetarian fare" is a contradiction? Long the target of unfair ridicule, vegetarian cuisine too often gets a bum rap.

To dispel this negative myth, we've created our new collection of recipes, featuring a treasure trove of more than 250 diverse, delectable meatless recipes that showcase fresh, seasonal ingredients in imaginative ways. Not just for vegetarians, it's an invaluable resource for anyone looking to expand his or her cooking repertoire.

We've divided the book into 9 chapters, each focused on a single food category, but you will find plenty of crossover between them. While Creamy Walnut Toss (page 168) appears in the Seeds & Nuts chapter (page 146), it wouldn't be out of place in either the Pasta (page 82) or Eggs & Cheese (page 176) chapters. Our index is the key, helping you search and find whatever type of recipe or ingredient you're seeking.

A greener life is more attainable now than ever before. For many, adopting a meat-free diet, even part-time, is becoming a mainstream way of life. On restaurant menus and grocery store shelves, and in the recipe collection you hold in your hands, appealing vegetarian options are much more readily available. And through these pages, we hope to encourage and empower you to hone your own creative cooking style.

– Alison Kent, editor

[CONTENTS

[VEGETARIAN
[KNOW-HOW

Vegetarian Types

There are several classifications of vegetarianism. Choosing the type that suits your needs will help you plan meals and ensure that you meet nutritional requirements. They include:

VEGETARIAN: Diet is based on vegetables, fruits, beans, grains, nuts and soy foods. This is a catch-all term.

VEGAN: Avoids all foods of animal origin, including eggs, dairy, gelatin and honey. Many also refrain from eating foods that are processed using animal products, such as sugar and some wines.

LACTO-OVO VEGETARIAN: Does not eat meat but does include eggs and dairy products. The majority of vegetarians in North America are this type. There are also two sub-categories:
Lacto-Vegetarian: Includes dairy products, but no eggs.
Ovo-Vegetarian: Includes eggs, but no dairy.

FLEXITARIAN OR SEMI-VEGETARIAN: Though not truly vegetarian, primarily eats meatless meals but includes chicken, meat, fish or seafood on occasion. Some fall into a sub-category:
Pesco-Vegetarian or **Pescetarian:** Includes fish and seafood, but not chicken or meat.

Vegetarian Protein Sources

GRAINS: Wheat, including pasta (which gets its own chapter, page 82); oats; millet; rice; and quinoa provide almost half of the world's protein. Choosing whole-grain versions also provides iron, zinc, B vitamins and fibre.

BEANS AND LEGUMES: Any plant that has seeds in pods, such as peas, lentils, chickpeas and beans, including peanuts (see Seeds & Nuts, page 146), is a legume. Legumes not only are high in protein but also provide iron and fibre. Soybeans are also legumes, so products made from them fall into this category, including tofu, TVP and tempeh. Because soy products are so important in most vegetarians' diets, they have their own dedicated chapter (page 112).

EGGS AND DAIRY: When following an ovo- or lacto-vegetarian diet, eggs and dairy products are good sources of complete protein. These also provide a source of vitamin B_{12}.

NUTS AND SEEDS: Often considered high-fat snack foods, nuts and seeds actually are a good source of protein and unsaturated and essential fats. When meat is eliminated from the diet, fat intake generally decreases, so upping your nut intake is a good thing.

VEGETABLES: While vegetables are not complete sources of protein, they do contain some of the amino acids needed to build protein.

Vegetarian Must-Have Nutrients

According to the Dietitians of Canada, appropriately planned vegetarian diets are healthy and nutritionally adequate, and may help prevent cancer, diabetes and heart disease. They also note that vegetarians tend to consume less cholesterol and saturated fat but consume more beneficial fibre, vitamins and antioxidants than their meat-eating peers. If that's not reason enough to consider eating more meatless meals, think about the money you'll save buying beans or soy instead of steak!

Planning a vegetarian diet does take some knowledge. When you remove meat, chicken and fish from your diet, you'll have to learn how to replace the missing protein, vitamins and minerals. By using meat alternatives, such as beans and lentils (especially in combination with whole grains), soy, tofu, nuts and seeds (and eggs and dairy in some cases), you should have no problem meeting all of your protein requirements. Vitamin and mineral intake may be trickier, so here are some helpful tips.

VITAMIN B$_{12}$. Since this essential nutrient is mostly found in animal-based foods, such as meat, dairy and eggs, strict vegetarians have to find alternative sources. Good choices include fortified soy beverages, fortified "mock meats" (such as veggie burgers), nutritional yeast and vitamin supplements.

CALCIUM. Vegetarians who consume two to three servings of dairy products daily will probably consume sufficient calcium. Those who restrict dairy will have to increase their intake of calcium-rich foods by including leafy greens, almonds, sesame seeds, beans, figs or calcium-fortified beverages. Supplements may also be necessary.

IRON. The richest source of well-absorbed iron is meat, so vegetarians need to look for alternatives. Fortified breakfast cereals, legumes (chickpeas; lentils; and navy, lima and kidney beans), oatmeal, firm tofu, dried apricots and pumpkin seeds all contain iron. Pair any food from this list with vitamin C–filled strawberries, potatoes, tomatoes, sweet peppers or citrus fruit to help boost iron absorption.

ZINC. An essential mineral in the diet, zinc is found in ample amounts in meat. To get enough, vegetarians can choose these foods: beans and chickpeas, soy nuts, cashews, pumpkin and sunflower seeds, almonds and yogurt.

Seeing a registered dietitian is a great first step toward planning a balanced diet. He or she can help ensure that you meet all your nutrient needs. You can find a dietitian in your area by visiting dietitians.ca/find.

DID YOU KNOW?

Many people choose to become vegetarian because of their growing concern for the environment. They believe that raising animals for the sole purpose of using their meat as food is an inefficient, planet-harming process. While animals eat large quantities of grain, they only produce small amounts of meat, dairy products or eggs in return. In fact, it can take up to 7¼ kg (16 lb) of grain to produce just 500 g (1 lb) of meat.

Choosing a diet based on vegetables, beans and grains is less draining on the food supply and on the earth, and cutting back on meat consumption is one way many environmentalists help protect the planet.

PULSES & BEANS

Black Bean, Chickpea
& Avocado Salad
(page 23)

Lentil Feta Salad

Prep: 20 minutes   **Cook:** 25 minutes   **Makes:** 6 servings

½ cup (125 mL) **slivered almonds**

1 cup (250 mL) **dried green lentils,** rinsed and drained

2 cloves **garlic**

¼ cup (60 mL) **extra-virgin olive oil**

3 tbsp (45 mL) **red wine vinegar**

1 tbsp (15 mL) finely chopped **fresh oregano**

¼ tsp (1 mL) each **salt** and **pepper**

1½ cups (375 mL) diced seeded **cucumber**

1 cup (250 mL) halved **cherry** or grape **tomatoes**

½ cup (125 mL) diced **sweet** or red **onion,** rinsed and drained

2 tbsp (30 mL) chopped **fresh parsley**

¾ cup (175 mL) crumbled **feta cheese**

※ Rinsing onion in cold water helps remove some of its harsh raw flavours.

In small dry skillet, toast almonds over medium heat, stirring often, until golden, about 5 minutes.

Bring large pot of salted water to boil. Add lentils and garlic; reduce heat and simmer until tender, about 20 minutes. Drain and rinse in cold water; drain again. Discard garlic.

In large bowl, whisk together oil, vinegar, oregano, salt and pepper. Add lentils, cucumber, tomatoes, onion and parsley; toss to coat.

Stir in almonds and all but ¼ cup (60 mL) of the feta; sprinkle with remaining feta just before serving.

PER SERVING: about 305 cal, 14 g pro, 18 g total fat (5 g sat. fat), 25 g carb, 6 g fibre, 17 mg chol, 532 mg sodium. % RDI: 14% calcium, 29% iron, 6% vit A, 13% vit C, 89% folate.

PULSES & BEANS

Peasant Soup

Prep: 10 minutes   **Cook:** 35 minutes   **Makes:** 6 servings

✳ If you like, make this rustic soup with chickpeas, kidney beans or any other favourite legume. You can substitute 1 tbsp (15 mL) chopped fresh mint or dill for the dried mint; add along with the parsley. If desired, use a mixture of half water and half broth instead of just water.

2 tbsp (30 mL) **vegetable oil**

3 stalks **celery,** diced

2 **carrots,** diced

1 **onion,** diced

3 cloves **garlic,** minced

½ tsp (2 mL) **salt**

½ tsp (2 mL) **dried mint**

¼ tsp (1 mL) **turmeric**

1 can (28 oz/796 mL) **whole tomatoes**

⅓ cup (75 mL) **dried green lentils,** rinsed and drained

1 tbsp (15 mL) **tomato paste**

½ cup (125 mL) **mini shell pasta**

1 can (19 oz/540 mL) **bean medley,** drained and rinsed

2 tbsp (30 mL) chopped **fresh parsley**

In large saucepan or Dutch oven, heat oil over medium heat; fry celery, carrots, onion, garlic, salt, mint and turmeric, stirring occasionally, until softened, about 6 minutes.

Stir in tomatoes, breaking up with back of spoon; stir in lentils, tomato paste and 4½ cups (1.125 L) water. Bring to boil; reduce heat and simmer, covered, until lentils are tender, about 25 minutes.

Meanwhile, in large pot of boiling salted water, cook pasta until al dente, about 8 minutes. Drain and add to soup along with beans and parsley; simmer for 5 minutes.

PER SERVING: about 250 cal, 12 g pro, 6 g total fat (trace sat. fat), 39 g carb, 8 g fibre, 0 mg chol, 748 mg sodium, 951 mg potassium. % RDI: 7% calcium, 22% iron, 47% vit A, 38% vit C, 42% folate.

Cumin & Sesame–Scented Chickpea Soup

Prep: 10 minutes   **Cook:** 20 minutes   **Makes:** 6 servings

1 tbsp (15 mL) **olive oil**

1 large **onion,** thinly sliced

2 cloves **garlic,** minced

1 tsp (5 mL) **cumin seeds**

½ tsp (2 mL) **salt**

¼ tsp (1 mL) **pepper**

2 **carrots,** diced

1 can (19 oz/540 mL) **chickpeas,** drained and rinsed

3 cups (750 mL) **vegetable broth**

1 tbsp (15 mL) chopped **fresh mint** or parsley

1 tbsp (15 mL) **lemon juice**

1 tsp (5 mL) **sesame oil**

In large saucepan, heat oil over medium heat; fry onion, garlic, cumin seeds, salt and pepper, stirring occasionally, until onion is softened, about 5 minutes.

Add carrots; cook until starting to soften, about 5 minutes. Stir in chickpeas, broth and 1 cup (250 mL) water, scraping up any brown bits from bottom of pan; bring to boil. Reduce heat and simmer, covered, until carrots are tender, about 10 minutes.

In blender or food processor, purée 2 cups (500 mL) of the soup until smooth; stir back into pot. Stir in mint, lemon juice and sesame oil.

PER SERVING: about 135 cal, 4 g pro, 3 g total fat (1 g sat. fat), 23 g carb, 4 g fibre, 0 mg chol, 671 mg sodium, 256 mg potassium. % RDI: 4% calcium, 10% iron, 46% vit A, 12% vit C, 22% folate.

Kale & Navy Bean Soup

Prep: 20 minutes   **Cook:** 35 minutes   **Makes:** 8 to 10 servings

2 tbsp (30 mL) **olive oil**

1 large **onion,** diced

3 cloves **garlic,** minced

1½ tsp (7 mL) **ground coriander**

1 tsp (5 mL) **ground cumin**

½ tsp (2 mL) each **salt** and **pepper**

6 cups (1.5 L) **vegetable broth**

2 cups (500 mL) diced peeled **potato** (about 2)

2 cups (500 mL) diced peeled **rutabaga** or sweet potato (about half rutabaga or 1 large sweet potato)

2 cans (each 19 oz/540 mL) **navy beans** or white kidney beans, drained and rinsed

6 cups (1.5 L) shredded deveined **kale leaves**

½ cup (125 mL) chopped **fresh parsley**

2 tsp (10 mL) **lemon juice**

✳ For an added flavour boost, dollop a spoonful of basil pesto on each bowl of soup. No spinach? Replace with trimmed spinach or Swiss chard leaves.

In Dutch oven, heat oil over medium heat; fry onion, garlic, coriander, cumin, salt and pepper, stirring occasionally, until onion is softened, about 5 minutes.

Add broth, 4 cups (1 L) water, potato, rutabaga and beans; bring to boil. Reduce heat and simmer, covered, until vegetables are tender, about 20 minutes.

Add kale and parsley; simmer, covered, until kale is tender, about 10 minutes. Stir in lemon juice.

PULSES & BEANS

PER EACH OF 10 SERVINGS: about 202 cal, 10 g pro, 4 g total fat (1 g sat. fat), 35 g carb, 4 g fibre, 0 mg chol, 806 mg sodium, 672 mg potassium. % RDI: 12% calcium, 20% iron, 63% vit A, 92% vit C, 31% folate.

Lentil, Beans & Greens Soup

Prep: 15 minutes   **Stand:** 8 hours   **Cook:** 1¼ hours   **Makes:** 8 servings

✳ Garnish bowls with a drizzle of extra-virgin olive oil, a sprinkle of grated Parmesan cheese and a pinch of hot pepper flakes, to taste. You can replace the reserved bean cooking liquid with vegetable broth, water or a combination of both that adds up to 4 cups (1 L).

½ cup (125 mL) **dried fava beans** or lima beans

½ cup (125 mL) **dried kidney beans**

½ cup (125 mL) **dried romano beans**

½ cup (125 mL) **dried chickpeas**

1 tbsp (15 mL) **olive oil**

1 **onion**, diced

2 **carrots**, diced

2 stalks **celery**, diced

1 clove **garlic**, minced

1 tsp (5 mL) **fennel seeds**, crushed

1 tsp (5 mL) **salt**

4 **oil-packed sun-dried tomatoes**, drained and sliced

1 cup (250 mL) **dried green lentils**, rinsed and drained

5 cups (1.25 L) chopped **Swiss chard leaves** (about 1 bunch)

2 cups (500 mL) **cooked small pasta**, such as ditali or macaroni

Rinse and soak fava beans, kidney beans, romano beans and chickpeas separately overnight in 3 times their volumes of water. Drain and rinse.

In Dutch oven, bring 8 cups (2 L) water to boil; cook fava beans for 5 minutes. Add kidney beans; cook for 5 minutes. Add romano beans and chickpeas; reduce heat and simmer until tender, about 45 minutes. Reserving 4 cups (1 L) of the cooking liquid, drain.

In clean Dutch oven, heat oil over medium heat; fry onion, carrots and celery until softened, 5 to 6 minutes. Add garlic, fennel seeds, salt and tomatoes; cook for 2 minutes.

Add reserved cooking liquid and 6 cups (1.5 L) water; bring to boil. Add lentils; reduce heat and simmer for 10 minutes.

Add Swiss chard and cooked beans; simmer until chard is wilted and lentils are tender, about 10 minutes. Stir in pasta.

PER SERVING: about 375 cal, 21 g pro, 7 g total fat (2 g sat. fat) 59 g carb, 12 g fibre, 5 mg chol, 393 mg sodium, 1,375 mg potassium. % RDI: 10% calcium, 59% iron, 39% vit A, 13% vit C, 170% folate.

DRIED BEANS

Most dried legumes (or beans) – except lentils – need to be soaked before cooking. Here are some guidelines.

SOAKING & COOKING

• Rinse and soak dried beans overnight in 3 times their volume of water. Or for the quick-soak method, bring to boil and boil gently for 2 minutes. Remove from heat and let stand, covered, for 1 hour. Drain.

• In saucepan, cover beans again with 3 times their volume of water; bring to boil. Reduce heat and simmer, covered, until tender, 30 to 80 minutes depending on bean variety (see Cooking Times, right). Drain, reserving cooking liquid to use in recipes.

• Do not add salt to the bean water until the very end of cooking. Salt will prevent the beans from absorbing water and becoming tender (again, lentils are the exception).

YIELDS

• Typically, 1 cup (250 mL) dried beans simmers into about 2 cups (500 mL) cooked beans (or up to ½ cup/ 125 mL more, depending on bean variety).

COOKING TIMES

• Cooking times vary among dried beans. The soaking method also changes cooking time: count on 5 to 10 minutes less cooking time if using the quick-soak method.

• Start checking beans, regardless of soaking method, by tasting them about 10 minutes before suggested cooking time, then every 5 minutes thereafter. A well-cooked bean is tender and easy to squash in your mouth.

• Black beans: 30 minutes
• Black-eyed peas: 35 minutes
• Lima beans: 40 minutes
• Navy beans: 40 minutes
• Chickpeas: 45 minutes
• Romano beans: 45 minutes
• Fava beans: 50 minutes
• Kidney beans (white and red): 50 minutes
• Large lima beans: 55 minutes

Squash, Corn & Lima Bean Soup

Prep: 10 minutes   **Cook:** 25 minutes   **Makes:** 6 servings

✳ Squeeze a lemon wedge into each bowl of soup to add fresh flavour.

2 tbsp (30 mL) **vegetable** or olive **oil**

2 **leeks** (white and light green parts only), chopped

2 cloves **garlic,** minced

1 tbsp (15 mL) chopped **fresh thyme**

½ tsp (2 mL) each **salt** and **pepper**

3 cups (750 mL) **vegetable broth**

2 cups (500 mL) cubed peeled **butternut squash**

1 cup (250 mL) **frozen lima beans** or shelled soybeans (edamame), thawed

1 **sweet red pepper,** diced

1 cup (250 mL) cooked **corn kernels**

In large saucepan or Dutch oven, heat oil over medium heat; fry leeks, garlic, thyme, salt and pepper, stirring occasionally, until leeks are softened, about 5 minutes.

Add broth, 3 cups (750 mL) water and squash; bring to boil. Reduce heat and simmer, covered, until squash is tender, about 15 minutes.

Add lima beans, red pepper and corn; simmer until pepper is tender, about 5 minutes.

PER SERVING: about 145 cal, 4 g pro, 5 g total fat (trace sat. fat), 24 g carb, 4 g fibre, 0 mg chol, 698 mg sodium. % RDI: 5% calcium, 12% iron, 42% vit A, 45% vit C, 17% folate.

Black Bean, Chickpea & Avocado Salad

Prep: 15 minutes   **Makes:** 4 to 6 servings

1 can (19 oz/540 mL) **black beans,** drained and rinsed

1 can (19 oz/540 mL) **chickpeas,** drained and rinsed

2 **green onions,** thinly sliced

2 **plum** or vine-ripened **tomatoes,** chopped

1 **sweet yellow** or red **pepper,** diced

1 **avocado,** peeled, pitted and diced

¼ cup (60 mL) chopped **fresh coriander**

1 tsp (5 mL) grated **lime rind**

¼ cup (60 mL) **lime juice**

¼ cup (60 mL) **vegetable** or olive **oil**

1 **jalapeño pepper,** seeded and minced

1 small clove **garlic,** minced

¼ tsp (1 mL) each **salt** and **pepper**

In large bowl, toss together black beans, chickpeas, onions, tomatoes, yellow pepper, avocado and coriander.

Whisk together lime rind and juice, oil, jalapeño, garlic, salt and pepper. Pour over bean mixture; toss to coat.

* With its jewel-toned colours, this salad takes hardly any time to put together. It's terrific on its own or over chilled cooked quinoa or rice. If making the salad ahead of time, add avocado just before serving.

PER EACH OF 6 SERVINGS: about 319 cal, 11 g pro, 16 g total fat (2 g sat. fat), 36 g carb, 8 g fibre, 0 mg chol, 387 mg sodium. % RDI: 4% calcium, 19% iron, 12% vit A, 95% vit C, 72% folate.

Bean & Wheat Berry Salad with Coriander Chili Dressing

Prep: 15 minutes   **Stand:** 15 minutes   **Cook:** 45 minutes   **Makes:** 4 servings

*If using pearl (polished) wheat berries, reduce cooking time to 25 minutes.

½ cup (125 mL) **soft wheat berries**

1 can (19 oz/540 mL) **black beans,** drained and rinsed

1 cup (250 mL) halved **cherry** or grape **tomatoes**

1 each **sweet red** and **yellow pepper,** diced

2 **green onions,** thinly sliced

1 **avocado,** peeled, pitted and diced

½ cup (125 mL) crumbled **feta cheese** or goat cheese

3 cups (750 mL) torn **romaine lettuce**

1 cup (250 mL) shredded deveined **kale leaves** or trimmed spinach

CORIANDER CHILI DRESSING:

¼ cup (60 mL) **olive oil**

2 tbsp (30 mL) chopped **fresh coriander**

2 tbsp (30 mL) **cider vinegar**

1 tbsp (15 mL) minced **shallot**

1 small clove **garlic,** minced

1 tsp (5 mL) minced **hot red** or green **pepper**

Pinch each **salt** and **pepper**

Bring large saucepan of salted water to boil. Add wheat berries; reduce heat and simmer, covered, until tender, 45 to 60 minutes. Drain and transfer to large bowl; let cool for 15 minutes.

CORIANDER CHILI DRESSING: Whisk together olive oil, coriander, vinegar, shallot, garlic, hot pepper, salt and pepper.

To wheat berries, add black beans, tomatoes, red and yellow peppers, onions, avocado and feta cheese. Pour Coriander Chili Dressing over top; toss to coat.

Divide lettuce and kale among plates; top with bean salad.

PER SERVING: about 439 cal, 15 g pro, 25 g total fat (6 g sat. fat), 47 g carb, 16 g fibre, 17 mg chol, 658 mg sodium. % RDI: 18% calcium, 29% iron, 60% vit A, 258% vit C, 85% folate.

Warm Black-Eyed Pea & Fennel Salad

Prep: 10 minutes   **Cook:** 10 minutes   **Makes:** 6 to 8 servings

¼ cup (60 mL) **extra-virgin olive oil** (approx)

1 cup (250 mL) thinly sliced **fennel** (about half bulb)

½ cup (125 mL) thinly sliced **celery**

3 cloves **garlic,** minced

½ tsp (2 mL) **dried thyme** (or 2 tsp/10 mL chopped fresh thyme)

½ tsp (2 mL) **salt**

3 cups (750 mL) **cooked black-eyed peas** (see Dried Beans, page 21)

¼ cup (60 mL) chopped **fresh parsley**

4 tsp (20 mL) **white wine vinegar** (approx)

* The warm peas deliciously absorb the dressing in this salad. To keep them moist, drizzle with additional oil and vinegar just before serving.

In shallow Dutch oven or skillet, heat 3 tbsp (45 mL) of the oil over medium heat; fry fennel, celery, garlic, thyme and salt, stirring occasionally, until softened and beginning to colour, about 8 minutes.

Stir in peas, parsley and 1 tbsp (15 mL) of the vinegar; cook for 2 minutes. Transfer to serving bowl; toss with remaining oil and vinegar, adding more if desired. Serve warm.

PER EACH OF 8 SERVINGS: about 142 cal, 5 g pro, 7 g total fat (1 g sat. fat), 15 g carb, 5 g fibre, 0 mg chol, 159 mg sodium. % RDI: 3% calcium, 14% iron, 2% vit A, 7% vit C, 64% folate.

Chickpea & Swiss Chard Curry

Prep: 10 minutes   **Cook:** 35 minutes   **Makes:** 4 servings

✳ Serve this quick curry over hot basmati rice, or with naan bread or pappadams.

2 tbsp (30 mL) **vegetable oil**

1 tsp (5 mL) **cumin seeds**

1 **onion,** finely chopped

2 **hot green peppers** (or 1 jalapeño pepper), seeded and chopped

2 tsp (10 mL) minced **fresh ginger**

3 cloves **garlic,** minced

¾ tsp (4 mL) **ground cumin**

¾ tsp (4 mL) **ground coriander**

½ tsp (2 mL) **garam masala**

2 tsp (10 mL) **tomato paste**

¼ tsp (1 mL) **cayenne pepper**

¼ tsp (1 mL) **turmeric**

1 cup (250 mL) chopped drained **canned whole tomatoes**

½ tsp (2 mL) **salt**

1 can (19 oz/540 mL) **chickpeas,** drained and rinsed

4 cups (1 L) chopped **Swiss chard leaves**

In large saucepan, heat oil over medium heat; fry cumin seeds until beginning to pop, about 1 minute. Add onion and hot peppers; cook until onion is softened, about 8 minutes. Add ginger and garlic; cook for 1 minute. Add ground cumin and coriander; cook until fragrant, about 2 minutes. Add garam masala; cook for 1 minute. Add tomato paste, cayenne and turmeric; cook for 1 minute.

Add tomatoes and salt; cook, stirring, until very soft, about 3 minutes. Stir in 1¼ cups (300 mL) water; bring to boil. Add chickpeas; reduce heat and simmer for 10 minutes. Stir in Swiss chard; simmer, covered, until tender, 4 to 5 minutes.

PER SERVING: about 260 cal, 10 g pro, 9 g total fat (1 g sat. fat), 39 g carb, 10 g fibre, 0 mg chol, 946 mg sodium, 1,269 mg potassium. % RDI: 15% calcium, 46% iron, 52% vit A, 72% vit C, 40% folate.

Vegetarian Chili Fries
(page 30)

Vegetarian Chili Fries

Prep: 20 minutes   **Stand:** 5 minutes   **Cook:** 1½ hours   **Makes:** 6 servings

✳ Whether appetizer-size or as a main course, oven-baked chili fries are a crowd-pleaser at any gathering. Omit the cheese and sour cream garnishes for a vegan dish.

3 lb (1.5 kg) **baking potatoes** (about 6), scrubbed
3 tbsp (45 mL) **olive oil**
½ tsp (2 mL) **salt**
¼ tsp (1 mL) **pepper**

CHILI:

2 tbsp (30 mL) **olive oil**
¼ cup (60 mL) diced **onion**
¼ cup (60 mL) diced **celery**
¼ cup (60 mL) diced **carrot**
2 cloves **garlic,** minced
1 tsp (5 mL) **chili powder**
1 tsp (5 mL) **paprika**

¼ tsp (1 mL) **hot pepper flakes**
¼ tsp (1 mL) each **salt** and **pepper**
1 can (28 oz/796 mL) **diced tomatoes**
1 can (19 oz/540 mL) **red kidney beans,** drained and rinsed

GARNISH:

¾ cup (175 mL) shredded **Cheddar cheese**
½ cup (125 mL) **sour cream**
¼ cup (60 mL) thinly sliced **green onions** (green parts only)

CHILI: In saucepan, heat oil over medium heat; fry onion, celery and carrot until softened, about 5 minutes. Add garlic, chili powder, paprika, hot pepper flakes, salt and pepper; cook for 2 minutes. Add tomatoes; bring to boil. Reduce heat and simmer, stirring occasionally, for 12 minutes. Add beans; simmer, stirring occasionally, until slightly thickened, about 12 minutes. Cover and keep warm.

Meanwhile, cut potatoes lengthwise into ½-inch (1 cm) thick slices. Cut lengthwise into ½-inch (1 cm) wide sticks. Soak in cold water for 5 minutes. Drain; pat dry.

Toss together potatoes, oil, salt and pepper; spread on 2 parchment paper–lined baking sheets. Bake in 425°F (220°C) oven, turning once, until crisp and golden, about 50 minutes. Divide among 6 dishes.

GARNISH: Top fries with Chili; sprinkle with cheese. Dollop with sour cream; sprinkle with green onions.

PER SERVING: about 456 cal, 14 g pro, 20 g total fat (6 g sat. fat), 60 g carb, 11 g fibre, 22 mg chol, 813 mg sodium, 1,517 mg potassium. % RDI: 20% calcium, 33% iron, 20% vit A, 65% vit C, 47% folate.

SUPER BEANS

The mighty bean may be small, but it holds a power-packed combination of nutrients.

• Beans are loaded with heart-protective vitamins and minerals, such as potassium and folate, which help combat high blood pressure and high homocysteine levels, respectively. Homocysteine is an amino acid found in the blood; too-high levels are linked to a higher risk of heart disease.

• Beans are high in fibre, providing about half your daily needs in 1 cup (250 mL). In particular, beans are rich in soluble fibre, which can help lower cholesterol levels.

• As "good carbs," beans have a low glycemic index rating, which means they can help slow digestion and balance blood sugar levels.

• High in protein, beans are an ideal alternative for vegetarian meals. Replacing fatty meats with vegetarian protein sources such as beans can help cut harmful saturated fat, further protecting your heart.

• Beans are rich in antioxidants, which can protect the heart against the harmful damage caused by free radicals (compounds produced in response to cellular breakdown, tobacco and other pollutants). The darker the bean, the more antioxidants, so choose red kidney beans over white. A ½-cup (125 mL) serving of red kidney beans provides more antioxidants than 1 cup (250 mL) of blueberries, cranberries or strawberries.

• People who eat beans at least four times per week have a 22 per cent lower risk of heart disease than individuals who consume beans less than once a week, so stock up on these nutrient powerhouses for optimal heart health.

Maple-Baked Beans

Prep: 15 minutes **Stand:** 8 hours **Cook:** 4 hours
Makes: about 8 cups (2 L), or 8 servings

✳ This classic comforting dish is made all the better with the sweet touches of apple, molasses and maple syrup. Sop up every bit of saucy goodness with Cheddar Herbed Skillet Cornbread (page 264).

3 cups (750 mL) **dried navy beans**

2 tbsp (30 mL) **vegetable oil**

1 **onion,** diced

1 **Granny Smith apple,** peeled and diced

2 cloves **garlic,** minced

1 tbsp (15 mL) **dry mustard**

2 tsp (10 mL) **chili powder**

½ tsp (2 mL) **salt**

Pinch **cayenne pepper**

2 cups (500 mL) **bottled strained tomatoes** (passata)

⅓ cup (75 mL) **maple syrup**

3 tbsp (45 mL) **cider vinegar**

2 tbsp (30 mL) **fancy molasses**

1½ cups (375 mL) **bean cooking liquid,** vegetable broth or water

Rinse and soak beans overnight in 3 times their volume of water. Drain and rinse.

In saucepan, cover beans again with 3 times their volume of water; bring to boil. Reduce heat and simmer, covered, until tender, about 40 minutes. Drain, reserving cooking liquid.

In saucepan, heat oil over medium heat; fry onion, apple, garlic, mustard, chili powder, salt and cayenne until softened, about 8 minutes.

Stir in strained tomatoes, maple syrup, vinegar and molasses; bring to boil. Reduce heat and simmer, covered, for 10 minutes. Scrape into food processor; add bean cooking liquid and purée until smooth.

In bean pot or 16-cup (4 L) casserole, combine beans with sauce. Bake, covered, in 300°F (150°C) oven for 2 hours. Uncover and bake until thickened, about 1 hour.

PER SERVING: about 374 cal, 16 g pro, 6 g total fat (1 g sat. fat), 70 g carb, 14 g fibre, 2 mg chol, 174 mg sodium. % RDI: 14% calcium, 44% iron, 6% vit A, 16% vit C, 116% folate.

Vegetable Lentil Gardener's Pie

Prep: 20 minutes   **Cook:** 1½ hours   **Makes:** 8 to 10 servings

2 tbsp (30 mL) **olive oil**

1 large **onion,** diced

1 stalk **celery,** diced

1 **carrot,** diced

3 cloves **garlic,** minced

1½ cups (375 mL) **dried brown** or green **lentils,** rinsed and drained

1 pkg (340 g) **precooked soy protein mixture** (such as Yves Veggie Ground Round)

2 tsp (10 mL) **ground cumin**

2 tsp (10 mL) **dried oregano**

1 tsp (5 mL) each **salt** and **pepper**

1 can (28 oz/796 mL) **crushed tomatoes**

⅔ cup (150 mL) **vegetable broth**

½ cup (125 mL) **dry white wine** or vegetable broth

2 **zucchini,** diced

2 lb (1 kg) **russet potatoes** (about 4)

2 lb (1 kg) **sweet potatoes** (about 4)

⅓ cup (75 mL) **milk**

3 tbsp (45 mL) **butter**

1½ cups (375 mL) grated **old Cheddar cheese**

2 **green onions,** thinly sliced

In Dutch oven, heat oil over medium heat; fry diced onion, celery, carrot and garlic until softened, 6 minutes. Stir in lentils, soy protein, cumin, oregano, and half each of the salt and pepper; cook for 3 minutes.

Stir in tomatoes, broth and wine; bring to boil. Reduce heat and simmer, covered and stirring occasionally, for 20 minutes. Add zucchini; cook, covered and stirring often, until thickened and lentils are tender, about 30 minutes.

Meanwhile, peel and cut russet and sweet potatoes into 2-inch (5 cm) chunks. In large saucepan of boiling salted water, cook potatoes, covered, until tender, about 20 minutes. Drain and return to dry saucepan; mash together with milk, butter and remaining salt and pepper. Stir in ½ cup (125 mL) of the cheese.

Scrape lentil mixture into 13- x 9-inch (3 L) baking dish; spread mashed potatoes over top. Sprinkle with remaining cheese and green onions. Bake in 375°F (190°C) oven until bubbly, about 30 minutes.

PER EACH OF 10 SERVINGS: about 429 cal, 23 g pro, 13 g total fat (6 g sat. fat), 58 g carb, 11 g fibre, 28 mg chol, 1,073 mg sodium, 1,387 mg potassium. % RDI: 24% calcium, 54% iron, 157% vit A, 55% vit C, 85% folate.

✳ You can make this casserole up to the point of spreading the mashed potatoes on top, then refrigerate it for up to a day. Cover with foil and bake for 45 minutes, then uncover, sprinkle with cheese and green onions and continue baking for 30 minutes. If cheese isn't golden brown by end of baking time, broil, watching closely, until it is, about 2 minutes.

Moroccan Vegetable Pie with Chickpea Crust

Prep: 30 minutes   **Stand:** 20 minutes   **Cook:** 1¼ hours   **Makes:** 6 servings

✳ For this pie, home-cooked chickpeas give the best flavour and texture. And they're easy to prepare – see Dried Beans, page 21.

2 tbsp (30 mL) **vegetable oil**

1 each **onion** and **carrot,** diced

1 clove **garlic,** minced

1 tsp (5 mL) **cinnamon**

½ tsp (2 mL) each **ground coriander** and **ground cumin**

½ tsp (2 mL) each **salt** and **pepper**

¼ tsp (1 mL) **cayenne pepper**

1 **sweet yellow** or red **pepper,** diced

1 **zucchini,** diced

3 cups (750 mL) small **cauliflower florets**

1 cup (250 mL) rinsed drained **cooked chickpeas**

1 cup (250 mL) **bottled strained tomatoes** (passata)

1 tbsp (15 mL) **lemon juice**

1 cup (250 mL) **frozen peas,** thawed

2 tbsp (30 mL) chopped **fresh coriander** or parsley

2 tbsp (30 mL) **almond butter** or natural peanut butter

CHICKPEA CRUST:

1 cup (250 mL) rinsed drained **cooked chickpeas**

⅓ cup (75 mL) cold **unsalted butter,** cubed

3 tbsp (45 mL) **cold water**

1 tsp (5 mL) **salt**

½ tsp (2 mL) **ground cumin**

½ tsp (2 mL) **turmeric**

1½ cups (375 mL) **all-purpose flour**

1 tbsp (15 mL) **milk**

In large saucepan, heat oil over medium heat; fry onion, carrot, garlic, cinnamon, ground coriander, cumin, salt, pepper and cayenne, stirring, until softened, 5 minutes. Add yellow pepper, zucchini, cauliflower and chickpeas; cook, stirring, until pepper is softened, 8 minutes. Add tomatoes and lemon juice. Reduce heat; simmer, covered, until tender, 20 minutes. Stir in peas, fresh coriander and almond butter; let cool.

CHICKPEA CRUST: Meanwhile, in food processor, pulse chickpeas, butter, water, salt, cumin and turmeric until crumbly. Pulse in flour.

Turn out onto floured surface; knead until smooth, 2 minutes. Cut in half; roll out each to 10-inch (25 cm) circle. Fit 1 into 9-inch (23 cm) pie plate; spoon in vegetable mixture. Lightly brush edge with milk. Top with remaining pastry; trim edge. Using fork, press edges to seal. Brush with milk; cut steam vents in top. Bake in bottom third of 400°F (200°C) oven until golden, 40 minutes. Let stand for 5 minutes before cutting.

PER SERVING: about 431 cal, 11 g pro, 20 g total fat (7 g sat. fat), 54 g carb, 8 g fibre, 32 mg chol, 1,051 mg sodium. % RDI: 8% calcium, 29% iron, 44% vit A, 103% vit C, 59% folate.

Lima Beans with Tomatoes & Sage

Prep: 10 minutes **Stand:** 8 hours **Cook:** 1 hour **Makes:** 4 servings

2 cups (500 mL) **dried lima beans**

1 tbsp (15 mL) **extra-virgin olive oil**

1 **onion,** sliced

6 cloves **garlic,** sliced

2 tbsp (30 mL) finely chopped **fresh parsley**

4 tsp (20 mL) finely chopped **fresh sage**

1¼ tsp (6 mL) **salt**

½ tsp (2 mL) **pepper**

1½ lb (750 g) **tomatoes** (about 4), peeled, seeded and diced

＊ To peel tomatoes, cut X in bottom of each, then immerse in boiling water until skins loosen, about 30 seconds. Drain and chill in ice water; drain again and slip off skins.

Rinse and soak beans overnight in 3 times their volume of water. Drain and rinse.

In large saucepan, cover beans again with 3 times their volume of water; bring to boil. Reduce heat and simmer until tender, about 40 minutes. Drain.

In saucepan, heat oil over medium heat; fry onion, garlic, half of the parsley, the sage, salt and pepper, stirring occasionally, until onion is softened, about 5 minutes.

Add ½ cup (125 mL) water, tomatoes and beans; simmer until tomatoes break down, about 10 minutes. Sprinkle with remaining parsley.

PER SERVING: about 419 cal, 24 g pro, 5 g total fat (1 g sat. fat), 74 g carb, 23 g fibre, 0 mg chol, 1,383 mg sodium. % RDI: 10% calcium, 54% iron, 10% vit A, 52% vit C, 195% folate.

PULSES & BEANS

Black Bean Quesadillas

Prep: 20 minutes   **Cook:** 25 minutes   **Makes:** 4 servings

* As a simple-yet-satisfying weeknight main or snack for a crowd, this recipe is destined to become a mainstay.

2 tsp (10 mL) **vegetable oil**

1 **onion,** chopped

1 **sweet green pepper,** diced

1 tbsp (15 mL) **chili powder**

½ tsp (2 mL) **ground cumin**

¼ tsp (1 mL) each **salt** and **pepper**

1 can (19 oz/540 mL) **black beans,** drained and rinsed

1 cup (250 mL) **salsa**

½ cup (125 mL) **cooked corn kernels**

4 large (10-inch/25 cm) **flour tortillas**

2 cups (500 mL) shredded **old Cheddar cheese**

½ cup (125 mL) **light sour cream**

¼ cup (60 mL) diced **pickled jalapeño peppers** (optional)

In large skillet, heat oil over medium heat; fry onion, green pepper, chili powder, cumin, salt and pepper, stirring occasionally, until onion is softened, about 8 minutes.

Add black beans, salsa and corn; cook, stirring often, until heated through, about 5 minutes.

Evenly spoon bean mixture over half of each tortilla; sprinkle with cheese. Fold uncovered half over top and press lightly. Bake on greased large baking sheet in 425°F (220°C) oven, turning once, until golden, 10 to 15 minutes. Cut into wedges; serve with sour cream, and jalapeños (if using).

PER SERVING: about 644 cal, 31 g pro, 28 g total fat (14 g sat. fat), 70 g carb, 10 g fibre, 64 mg chol, 1,201 mg sodium. % RDI: 51% calcium, 39% iron, 31% vit A, 62% vit C, 79% folate.

Falafels

Prep: 25 minutes   **Stand:** 6 hours   **Cook:** 10 minutes
Makes: 24 pieces or 8 sandwiches

1 cup (250 mL) **dried chickpeas**

¾ cup (175 mL) chopped **onion**

2 tbsp (30 mL) chopped **fresh parsley**

2 cloves **garlic,** minced

½ cup (125 mL) **all-purpose flour**

4 tsp (20 mL) **ground cumin**

2 tsp (10 mL) **baking powder**

2 tsp (10 mL) **lemon juice**

1½ tsp (7 mL) **salt**

Vegetable oil for frying

24 **mini-pitas,** tops cut off, or 4 large pitas with pockets, cut in half

Thinly sliced **radishes**

Shredded **lettuce**

TAHINI YOGURT SAUCE:

⅔ cup (150 mL) **Balkan-style plain yogurt**

½ cup (125 mL) **tahini**

¼ cup (60 mL) **lemon juice**

2 tbsp (30 mL) minced **fresh parsley**

2 tbsp (30 mL) **extra-virgin olive oil**

¼ tsp (1 mL) **salt**

¼ tsp (1 mL) **cayenne pepper**

In bowl, pour enough cold water over chickpeas to cover by 1 inch (2.5 cm); soak for 4 hours or up to 24 hours. Drain well.

In food processor, coarsely chop chickpeas, onion, parsley and garlic, about 30 seconds. Add flour, cumin, baking powder, lemon juice and salt; pulse until blended, 10 seconds. Shape by heaping 1 tbsp (15 mL) into 24 balls; flatten to ½-inch (1 cm) thickness. Arrange in single layer on waxed paper–lined tray; refrigerate for 2 hours or up to 12 hours.

Pour enough oil into wok or Dutch oven to come about 2 inches (5 cm) up side; heat to 350°F (180°C) using deep-fry thermometer. In batches, gently drop falafels into hot oil. Deep-fry, turning once, until golden and cooked through, 3 minutes. Drain on paper towel–lined tray. (To reheat, bake on greased baking sheet in 350°F/180°C oven for 5 to 10 minutes.)

TAHINI YOGURT SAUCE: Meanwhile, whisk together yogurt, tahini, lemon juice, parsley, oil, salt and cayenne.

Stuff pitas with falafels (1 for each mini; 3 for each large pita half), radish slices and lettuce. Drizzle with Tahini Yogurt Sauce.

PER PIECE: 138 cal, 4 g pro, 8 g total fat (1 g sat. fat), 14 g carb, 2 g fibre, 1 mg chol, 235 mg sodium. % RDI: 4% calcium, 10% iron, 1% vit A, 3% vit C, 22% folate.

PULSES & BEANS

Roasted Red Pepper Hummus on Tortillas

Prep: 10 minutes   **Makes:** 4 servings

4 leaves **leaf lettuce**

4 large (10-inch/25 cm) **whole wheat tortillas**

1⅓ cups (325 mL) **Roasted Red Pepper Hummus** (recipe below)

½ cup (125 mL) grated **carrots**

½ cup (125 mL) thinly sliced **cucumber**

½ cup (125 mL) **alfalfa sprouts**

Place 1 lettuce leaf on each tortilla; spread each with ⅓ cup (75 mL) of the hummus. Sprinkle with carrots, cucumber and sprouts. Tuck sides over filling; roll up from end. Cut each diagonally in half.

PER SERVING: about 330 cal, 10 g pro, 13 g total fat (2 g sat. fat), 54 g carb, 8 g fibre, 0 mg chol, 628 mg sodium. % RDI: 6% calcium, 19% iron, 47% vit A, 60% vit C, 33% folate.

ROASTED RED PEPPER HUMMUS

Prep: 5 minutes   **Makes:** 2 cups (500 mL)

* Spread and roll in a tortilla or pita, or serve hummus as a dip for veggies and crackers.

1 can (19 oz/540 mL) **chickpeas,** drained and rinsed

½ cup (125 mL) drained **bottled roasted red peppers**

¼ cup (60 mL) **lemon juice**

¼ cup (60 mL) **tahini**

¼ cup (60 mL) **olive oil**

2 cloves **garlic,** minced

¼ tsp (1 mL) each **salt** and **pepper**

In food processor, purée together chickpeas, red peppers, lemon juice, tahini, oil, garlic, salt and pepper until smooth, adding a little water to thin if desired.

PER 1 TBSP (15 mL): about 38 cal, trace pro, 2 g total fat (trace sat. fat), 4 g carb, 1 g fibre, 0 mg chol, 65 mg sodium. % RDI: 1% calcium, 1% iron, 1% vit A, 10% vit C, 4% folate.

Braised Romano Beans & Peppers

Prep: 20 minutes   **Stand:** 20 minutes   **Cook:** 2¾ hours
Makes: 6 to 8 servings

3 each **sweet red** and **yellow peppers**

¼ cup (60 mL) **olive oil**

2 **onions,** thinly sliced

3 cloves **garlic,** thinly sliced

1 tbsp (15 mL) chopped **fresh oregano** (or ½ tsp/2 mL dried)

¾ tsp (4 mL) **salt**

½ tsp (2 mL) **pepper**

¼ tsp (1 mL) **hot pepper flakes**

4 cups (1 L) **cooked romano beans** (see Dried Beans, page 21)

2 cups (500 mL) **bean cooking liquid,** vegetable broth or water

1 tsp (5 mL) **white wine vinegar**

¼ cup (60 mL) sliced **fresh basil leaves** or chopped parsley

Broil red and yellow peppers, turning often, until charred all over, about 20 minutes. Transfer to bowl; let stand, covered, for 15 minutes. Uncover; let cool enough to handle. Peel, seed and quarter peppers; thinly slice crosswise.

In Dutch oven, heat oil over medium heat; fry onions, garlic, oregano, salt, pepper and hot pepper flakes, stirring occasionally, until onions are softened, about 8 minutes. Stir in peppers, beans and bean cooking liquid.

Bake, covered, in 375°F (190°C) oven for 2 hours. Stir in vinegar; uncover and bake for 10 minutes. Stir in basil.

*This makes a fantastic side dish or main alongside a green salad and crusty bread. During warmer months, char the peppers on the barbecue instead. In a pinch, you can use drained bottled roasted red peppers, and you could substitute the same amount of rinsed drained canned romano or white kidney beans for the dried.

PER EACH OF 8 SERVINGS: about 218 cal, 9 g pro, 7 g total fat (1 g sat. fat), 31 g carb, 7 g fibre, 0 mg chol, 220 mg sodium. % RDI: 6% calcium, 18% iron, 18% vit A, 233% vit C, 92% folate.

Chickpea Panisse

Prep: 5 minutes   **Stand:** 1 hour   **Cook:** 30 minutes   **Makes:** about 48 pieces

* *Panisses* are like chickpea polenta fried into sticks – crispy on the outside, soft on the inside. Chickpea flour, called *besan,* is available in Indian and Asian grocery stores, and some supermarkets. Serve warm with your choice of the savoury dips opposite.

⅔ cup (150 mL) **olive oil**
¾ tsp (4 mL) **salt**
2¼ cups (550 mL) **chickpea flour**
¼ tsp (1 mL) **pepper**

In saucepan, heat 4 cups (1 L) water, 1 tbsp (15 mL) of the oil and ½ tsp (2 mL) of the salt over high heat until hot but not quite simmering. Reduce heat to medium and whisk in flour; cook, whisking constantly, for 2 minutes. Switch to wooden spoon or heatproof spatula; continue cooking, stirring constantly, until very thick and batter holds its shape, about 10 minutes.

Scrape into greased 8-inch (2 L) square metal cake pan; smooth top. Let cool until set, about 1 hour.

Invert onto cutting board. Cut in half, then crosswise into ⅓-inch (8 mm) wide sticks.

In large nonstick skillet, heat one-third of the remaining oil over medium-high heat; fry one-third of the sticks, turning once, until deep golden and crisp, 5 to 6 minutes. Transfer to paper towel–lined baking sheet; sprinkle with one-third of the remaining salt and one-third of the pepper. Keep warm in 200°F (100°C) oven; repeating with remaining oil, sticks salt and pepper.

PER PIECE: about 43 cal, 1 g pro, 3 g total fat (trace sat. fat), 3 g carb, 1 g fibre, 0 mg chol, 39 mg sodium, 37 mg potassium. % RDI: 1% iron, 6% folate.

PULSES & BEANS

CHIPOTLE DIP

Prep: 5 minutes   **Makes:** about ⅔ cup (150 mL)

⅓ cup (75 mL) **Balkan-style plain yogurt**

⅓ cup (75 mL) **light mayonnaise**

1 tbsp (15 mL) chopped **canned chipotle pepper** with adobo sauce

1 tsp (5 mL) **lemon juice**

Pinch each **salt** and **pepper**

Whisk together yogurt, mayonnaise, chipotle with adobo sauce, lemon juice, salt and pepper.

PER 1 TBSP (15 ML): about 31 cal, 1 g pro, 3 g total fat (1 g sat. fat), 1 g carb, 0 g fibre, 3 mg chol, 68 mg sodium, 21 mg potassium. % RDI: 1% calcium, 1% vit A.

CURRY DIP

Prep: 5 minutes   **Makes:** about ¾ cup (175 mL)

½ cup (125 mL) **Balkan-style plain yogurt**

⅓ cup (75 mL) **light mayonnaise**

1 tbsp (15 mL) **curry paste**

2 tsp (10 mL) **lemon juice**

Pinch each **salt** and **pepper**

Whisk together yogurt, mayonnaise, curry paste, lemon juice, salt and pepper.

PER 1 TBSP (15 ML): about 33 cal, trace pro, 3 g total fat (1 g sat. fat), 1 g carb, trace fibre, 3 mg chol, 84 mg sodium, 20 mg potassium. % RDI: 1% calcium.

PULSES & BEANS

[GRAINS

Sushi Vegetable Pizza
(page 80)

Barley Lentil Soup
(opposite) with Rye
Cracker Bread (page 263)

Barley Lentil Soup

Prep: 10 minutes   **Cook:** 45 minutes   **Makes:** 4 to 6 servings

1 tbsp (15 mL) **vegetable oil**

1 **onion**, diced

2 cloves **garlic**, minced

1 **carrot**, diced

1 stalk **celery**, diced

1 tbsp (15 mL) chopped **fresh thyme**

¼ tsp (1 mL) each **salt** and **pepper**

4 cups (1 L) **vegetable broth**

1 cup (250 mL) **dried brown** or green **lentils**, rinsed and drained

¼ cup (60 mL) **pot barley**

¼ cup (60 mL) chopped **fresh parsley**

TOPPING:

¼ cup (60 mL) **Balkan-style plain yogurt**

1 tbsp (15 mL) minced **fresh parsley**

In large saucepan, heat oil over medium heat; fry onion, garlic, carrot, celery, thyme, salt and pepper, stirring occasionally, until softened, about 5 minutes.

Add broth, 2 cups (500 mL) water, lentils and barley; bring to boil. Reduce heat and simmer, covered, until lentils and barley are tender, about 40 minutes. Stir in parsley.

TOPPING: Top each serving with yogurt; sprinkle with parsley.

* While you can omit the yogurt garnish for a vegan version, it adds a depth of flavour and tangy creaminess to this hearty soup.

GRAINS

PER EACH OF 6 SERVINGS: about 193 cal, 10 g pro, 3 g total fat (trace sat. fat), 32 g carb, 5 g fibre, 1 mg chol, 544 mg sodium. % RDI: 6% calcium, 29% iron, 40% vit A, 12% vit C, 83% folate.

Grilled Vegetable Couscous Salad

Prep: 12 minutes   **Stand:** 5 minutes   **Cook:** 10 minutes   **Makes:** 4 servings

3 tbsp (45 mL) **balsamic vinegar**

2 tbsp (30 mL) **basil pesto**

1 tbsp (15 mL) **extra-virgin olive oil**

½ tsp (2 mL) **pepper**

¾ cup (175 mL) **whole wheat couscous** or white couscous

¾ cup (175 mL) **boiling water**

1 can (19 oz/540 mL) **chickpeas,** drained and rinsed

1 **green onion,** sliced

1 large **eggplant**

1 large **zucchini**

1 **sweet yellow pepper,** quartered and seeded

1 cup (250 mL) halved **grape tomatoes** or cherry tomatoes

Whisk together vinegar, pesto, oil and pepper.

In large bowl, combine couscous with boiling water; let stand, covered, for 5 minutes. Fluff with fork. Fold in chickpeas and green onion.

Cut eggplant and zucchini lengthwise into ½-inch (1 cm) thick slices. Grill eggplant, zucchini and pepper, covered, on greased grill over medium-high heat, turning once, until tender, about 10 minutes.

Cut eggplant, zucchini and pepper into 2-inch (5 cm) wide pieces. Add grilled vegetables and tomatoes to couscous. Add pesto mixture; toss to coat.

PER SERVING: about 395 cal, 13 g pro, 8 g total fat (1 g sat. fat), 72 g carb, 14 g fibre, 0 mg chol, 385 mg sodium. % RDI: 7% calcium, 24% iron, 11% vit A, 93% vit C, 45% folate.

Wild Rice Mushroom Soup

Prep: 15 minutes   **Stand:** 35 minutes   **Cook:** 40 minutes   **Makes:** 6 servings

✱ This velvety, nutty-textured soup tastes almost too rich to be meatless, but it is! For a slightly thinner dairy-free version, replace butter with additional olive oil and replace cream with almond, rice or soy milk.

1 pkg (½ oz/14 g) **dried porcini mushrooms**
1 cup (250 mL) **boiling water**
2 tbsp (30 mL) **butter**
1 tbsp (15 mL) **vegetable oil**
4 cups (1 L) sliced **cremini mushrooms**
¾ tsp (4 mL) **salt**
¼ cup (60 mL) **brandy** or vegetable broth
2 cups (500 mL) diced **onions**

2 cups (500 mL) diced **celery**
2 cloves **garlic,** minced
1 tbsp (15 mL) chopped **fresh thyme**
¼ tsp (1 mL) **pepper**
2 cups (500 mL) **vegetable broth**
1½ cups (375 mL) **Cooked Wild Rice** (opposite)
¼ cup (60 mL) **whipping cream**

Soak porcinis in boiling water until softened, about 30 minutes. Reserving soaking liquid, strain; discard sediment. Chop porcinis.

In skillet, heat half of the butter with the oil over medium-high heat; sauté cremini and porcini mushrooms and ¼ tsp (1 mL) of the salt until golden, about 5 minutes.

Add brandy; cook until most of the liquid is evaporated, about 1 minute.

In large saucepan, melt remaining butter over medium heat; fry onions, celery, garlic, thyme, pepper and remaining salt, stirring often, until very soft, about 10 minutes.

Add reserved soaking liquid, broth and 2 cups (500 mL) water; bring to boil. Reduce heat and simmer, stirring occasionally, for 20 minutes. Stir in mushrooms; let cool slightly.

In blender, purée half of the soup; return to pan. Stir in wild rice and cream; bring to simmer over medium heat, stirring often. (To store, let cool for 30 minutes; refrigerate in airtight container for up to 2 days.)

PER SERVING: about 198 cal, 5 g pro, 10 g total fat (5 g sat. fat), 22 g carb, 4 g fibre, 26 mg chol, 1,018 mg sodium. % RDI: 5% calcium, 6% iron, 8% vit A, 12% vit C, 18% folate.

COOKED WILD RICE

Prep: 1 minute **Stand:** 5 minutes **Cook:** 45 minutes
Makes: 1½ cups (375 mL)

½ cup (125 mL) **wild rice**
½ tsp (2 mL) **salt**

In saucepan, bring 2 cups
(500 mL) water, wild rice and salt
to boil over high heat. Reduce heat
and simmer, covered, until most of
the rice is split and tender, about
45 minutes. Remove from heat; let
stand for 5 minutes. Drain. (Or, let
cool for 30 minutes; refrigerate in
airtight container for up to 2 days.)

PER ¼ CUP (60 mL): about 47 cal, 2 g
pro, trace total fat (0 g sat. fat), 10 g
carb, 1 g fibre, 0 mg chol, 195 mg
sodium. % RDI: 2% iron, 5% folate.

GRAINS

Wild Rice
Mushroom Soup
(page 52)

Fresh Quinoa Veggie Salad

Prep: 15 minutes   **Cook:** 25 minutes   **Makes:** 6 to 8 servings

* The light and nutty texture of quinoa makes this high-protein ancient New World grain ideal in salads. Use light-colour South American quinoa or the nutty brown quinoa harvested in Saskatchewan. No turnip? Replace with half a small bulb of fennel, diced.

2 cups (500 mL) **quinoa**

1 **carrot,** diced

1 stalk **celery,** diced

1 **white turnip,** peeled and diced

3 **plum tomatoes,** diced

1 cup (250 mL) diced **cucumber**

3 **green onions** (white parts only), thinly sliced

¼ cup (60 mL) chopped **fresh parsley**

2 tbsp (30 mL) chopped **fresh mint**

¼ cup (60 mL) **lemon juice**

1 tbsp (15 mL) **red wine vinegar**

1 clove **garlic,** minced

¾ tsp (4 mL) **salt**

¼ tsp (1 mL) **pepper**

Dash **hot pepper sauce**

⅓ cup (75 mL) **extra-virgin olive oil**

In fine sieve, rinse quinoa under cold running water; drain. In saucepan, combine quinoa, carrot, celery, turnip and 3½ cups (875 mL) water; bring to boil. Reduce heat and simmer until quinoa is tender and no liquid remains, about 20 minutes. Transfer to bowl; fluff with fork. Let cool.

Add tomatoes, cucumber, onions, parsley and mint.

Whisk together lemon juice, vinegar, garlic, salt, pepper and hot pepper sauce; whisk in oil. Add to salad; toss to coat.

PER EACH OF 8 SERVINGS: about 266 cal, 7 g pro, 12 g total fat (2 g sat. fat), 36 g carb, 4 g fibre, 0 mg chol, 258 mg sodium. % RDI: 5% calcium, 34% iron, 28% vit A, 35% vit C, 16% folate.

GRAINS

QUINOA:
AN ANCIENT GRAIN

A sacred food of the Incas, quinoa (pronounced KEEN-wah) provides a wide range of vitamins and minerals. It is considered a complete protein because it contains all eight of the essential amino acids we need for tissue development. A gluten-free grain, quinoa is higher in calcium, phosphorus, magnesium, potassium, iron, copper, manganese and zinc than corn, barley and wheat.

Quinoa is coated with a natural pest repellent called saponin, which can have a slightly bitter taste. To remove it before cooking, rinse well under cold running water in a fine sieve and drain.

Versatile, slightly nutty and chewy, quinoa can be used in place of rice in hot cereals, casseroles, soups, stews, salads and desserts. Ground quinoa can be used in breads, cookies, muffins and pasta. Look for it in grocery and health food stores.

Barley Mushroom Walnut Salad

Prep: 10 minutes   **Cook:** 30 minutes   **Makes:** 6 servings

1 cup (250 mL) **pearl barley**

¾ cup (175 mL) sliced **green beans**

⅓ cup (75 mL) chopped **walnuts**

2 tbsp (30 mL) **olive oil**

3 cups (750 mL) sliced **white mushrooms**

1 stalk **celery,** diced

LEMON DRESSING:

3 tbsp (45 mL) **extra-virgin olive oil**

3 tbsp (45 mL) **lemon juice**

2 tbsp (30 mL) minced **fresh parsley**

1 clove **garlic,** minced

1 **shallot** or 2 green onions, minced

1 tbsp (15 mL) **Dijon mustard**

¼ tsp (1 mL) each **salt** and **pepper**

In saucepan of boiling salted water, cook barley, covered, until tender, about 20 minutes. Add green beans; cook until tender-crisp, about 3 minutes. Drain and chill under cold water; drain and return to pot.

In dry skillet, toast walnuts over medium-low heat until fragrant, about 2 minutes; add to barley mixture.

In same skillet, heat oil over medium-high heat; sauté mushrooms until golden, about 4 minutes. Add to barley mixture along with celery.

LEMON DRESSING: Whisk together oil, lemon juice, parsley, garlic, shallot, mustard, salt and pepper; toss with barley mixture to coat.

PER SERVING: about 311 cal, 5 g pro, 20 g total fat (4 g sat. fat), 33 g carb, 4 g fibre, 9 mg chol, 211 mg sodium. % RDI: 4% calcium, 17% iron, 2% vit A, 15% vit C, 19% folate.

Bulgur & Mushroom–Stuffed Peppers

Prep: 20 minutes   **Stand:** 15 minutes   **Cook:** 1¾ hours   **Makes:** 4 servings

1⅓ cups (325 mL) **boiling water**

½ cup (125 mL) **bulgur**

4 **sweet green** or red **peppers**

2 tbsp (30 mL) **olive oil**

1 lb (500 g) **cremini** or white **mushrooms,** finely chopped

1 **onion,** diced

2 cloves **garlic,** minced

½ tsp (2 mL) each **salt** and **pepper**

½ cup (125 mL) grated **Parmesan cheese**

¼ cup (60 mL) toasted **pine nuts** or slivered almonds

2 tbsp (30 mL) chopped **fresh dill**

2 tbsp (30 mL) chopped **fresh parsley**

1 tbsp (15 mL) **lemon juice**

1½ cups (375 mL) halved **grape** or cherry **tomatoes**

In large bowl, pour boiling water over bulgur; let stand, covered, for 15 minutes. Drain and press out moisture; return to dry bowl.

Meanwhile, about 1 inch (2.5 cm) down from stem end, slice tops off peppers. Finely dice tops; scrape out ribs and seeds from peppers.

In large nonstick skillet, heat half of the oil over medium-high heat; sauté diced pepper tops, mushrooms, onion, garlic, salt and pepper until no liquid remains, about 10 minutes. Add to bulgur along with cheese, pine nuts, dill and parsley; toss to combine.

Spoon bulgur mixture into peppers, mounding if necessary. Place peppers in greased 8-inch (2 L) square glass baking dish. Drizzle with lemon juice; top with tomatoes. Drizzle with remaining oil. Add 2 tbsp (30 mL) water to pan.

Cover with foil; bake in 350°F (180°C) oven until peppers are almost tender, about 1 hour. Uncover and bake until tops are crusty, about 30 minutes.

PER SERVING: about 305 cal, 12 g pro, 17 g total fat (4 g sat. fat), 32 g carb, 7 g fibre, 11 mg chol, 494 mg sodium, 854 mg potassium. % RDI: 17% calcium, 19% iron, 11% vit A, 160% vit C, 25% folate.

GRAINS

Polenta with Mushroom Ragout

Prep: 10 minutes   **Cook:** 25 minutes   **Makes:** 4 servings

GRAINS

✳ Oyster or king oyster mushrooms, shiitake caps, cremini, white, enoki (don't quarter) or, when in season, morel mushrooms are just some of the many varieties that would make a fantastic mushroom ragout.

2 tbsp (30 mL) **extra-virgin olive oil**

1½ lb (750 mL) **mixed mushrooms,** quartered

1 **onion,** minced

2 cloves **garlic,** minced

1 tbsp (15 mL) minced **fresh thyme**

¼ tsp (1 mL) each **salt** and **pepper**

½ cup (125 mL) **dry white wine** or vegetable broth

1 tbsp (15 mL) **all-purpose flour**

1½ cups (375 mL) **vegetable broth**

¼ cup (60 mL) chopped **fresh parsley**

POLENTA:

3 cups (750 mL) **milk**

¼ tsp (1 mL) **salt**

1 cup (250 mL) **cornmeal**

¼ cup (60 mL) grated **Parmesan cheese**

In Dutch oven, heat oil over medium-high heat; sauté mushrooms, onion, garlic, thyme, salt and pepper until no liquid remains, about 8 minutes.

Add wine; cook, stirring, until evaporated, about 4 minutes.

Stir in flour to coat. Stir in broth; bring to boil. Reduce heat and simmer, stirring occasionally, until slightly thickened, about 10 minutes. Stir in parsley.

POLENTA: Meanwhile, in large saucepan, bring milk, salt and 1 cup (250 mL) water to boil. Whisk in cornmeal; reduce heat and simmer, stirring with wooden spoon, until thick enough to mound on spoon, about 15 minutes. Stir in Parmesan cheese. Serve ragout over polenta.

PER SERVING: about 375 cal, 15 g pro, 13 g total fat (4 g sat. fat), 48 g carb, 6 g fibre, 20 mg chol, 843 mg sodium. % RDI: 29% calcium, 18% iron, 16% vit A, 12% vit C, 48% folate.

Squash Couscous

Prep: 30 minutes   **Stand:** 20 minutes   **Cook:** 1¼ hours   **Makes:** 8 servings

4 cups (1 L) **vegetable broth**

1 **Spanish onion,** thinly sliced

1 tsp (5 mL) **ground ginger**

½ tsp (2 mL) **turmeric**

½ tsp (2 mL) each **salt** and **pepper**

½ cup (125 mL) **sultana raisins**

¼ cup (60 mL) **granulated sugar**

¼ cup (60 mL) **butter**

4 cups (1 L) **couscous**

1½ lb (750 g) **butternut squash**

2 **yellow** or green **zucchini**

2 cups (500 mL) **cooked chickpeas** (see Dried Beans, page 21), peeled if desired

2 tbsp (30 mL) chopped **fresh parsley**

Harissa (page 275)

* This steamed preparation takes a little longer than the instant method of making couscous that's familiar to most people, but the plumper, al dente texture is well worth the effort.

In steamer bottom, cover and bring broth, onion, ginger, turmeric, salt and pepper to boil; reduce heat and simmer, covered, for 30 minutes.

Add raisins, sugar and butter; simmer until liquid is reduced by one-third, raisins are plumped and onion is translucent, about 15 minutes.

Meanwhile, rinse couscous; drain. Transfer to bowl; let stand for 20 minutes. With hands, break up lumps. Line top of steamer with cheesecloth; pour in one-quarter of the couscous.

Meanwhile, peel and cut squash into 2-inch (5 cm) cubes. Halve zucchini lengthwise; cut into 2-inch (5 cm) pieces.

Add squash, zucchini and chickpeas to reduced broth mixture; set steamer top in place. Cover and steam for 5 minutes. Add remaining couscous to top; steam until fluffy, about 20 minutes.

Dump couscous onto centre of large platter or into shallow bowl; make well in centre. Using slotted spoon, arrange vegetables in well. Strain broth; pour over couscous. Sprinkle with parsley; serve with Harissa.

PER SERVING (WITHOUT HARISSA): about 575 cal, 18 g pro, 8 g total fat (4 g sat. fat), 109 g carb, 7 g fibre, 18 mg chol, 734 mg sodium. % RDI: 8% calcium, 21% iron, 55% vit A, 27% vit C, 45% folate.

Spiced Brown Rice Pilau with Eggplant

Prep: 20 minutes   **Stand:** 10 minutes   **Cook:** 1¼ hours   **Makes:** 6 servings

✳ Serve this fragrant East Indian dish with Spinach Raita (page 273), a refreshing palate cleanser. If you are adventurous, increase the number of hot peppers to taste.

1 **eggplant** (about 1 lb/500 g)

3 tbsp (45 mL) **vegetable oil**

1 tsp (5 mL) **salt**

2 cups (500 mL) **brown basmati rice**

5 **whole cloves**

5 **cardamom pods,** cracked

2 **bay leaves**

1 piece (3 inches/8 cm) **cassia bark** or cinnamon

1½ tsp (7 mL) **fennel seeds**

½ tsp (2 mL) **cumin seeds**

1 large **onion,** diced

3 cloves **garlic,** minced

1 **green hot pepper,** sliced (and seeded, if desired)

¼ cup (60 mL) minced **fresh coriander**

2 tbsp (30 mL) **curry paste**

2 tsp (10 mL) minced **fresh ginger**

2 **tomatoes,** each cut into 8 wedges

1 can (19 oz/540 mL) **chickpeas,** drained and rinsed

Coriander sprigs

Peel and cut eggplant into 1-inch (2.5 cm) cubes; toss with 1 tbsp (15 mL) of the oil and ¼ tsp (1 mL) of the salt. Roast on parchment paper–lined baking sheet in 450°F (230°C) oven until browned, about 20 minutes.

Meanwhile, soak rice in 3¾ cups (925 mL) warm water for 10 minutes. Reserving soaking water, drain.

In Dutch oven, heat remaining oil over medium heat; fry cloves, cardamom, bay leaves, cassia, and fennel and cumin seeds until crackling, about 30 seconds. Add onion; cook, stirring occasionally, until starting to colour, 5 to 6 minutes.

Add garlic, hot pepper, minced coriander, curry paste, ginger and remaining salt; cook until fragrant, about 2 minutes. Stir in rice until coated; stir in eggplant and tomatoes. Add reserved soaking water; bring to boil. Reduce heat and simmer, covered, for 30 minutes.

Stir in chickpeas; cook until rice is tender and no liquid remains, about 15 minutes. Fluff with fork. Garnish with coriander sprigs.

PER SERVING: about 440 cal, 10 g pro, 12 g total fat (1 g sat. fat), 73 g carb, 9 g fibre, 0 mg chol, 724 mg sodium. % RDI: 6% calcium, 17% iron, 7% vit A, 23% vit C, 29% folate.

Quinoa Cakes with Lemon Yogurt Sauce

Prep: 25 minutes   **Stand:** 1¼ hours   **Cook:** 35 minutes
Makes: about 8 servings

1½ cups (375 mL) **quinoa**

1½ cups (375 mL) **vegetable broth**

½ cup (125 mL) **olive oil**

Half **onion,** chopped

3 cloves **garlic,** minced

½ tsp (2 mL) **salt**

¼ tsp (1 mL) **pepper**

3 cups (750 mL) trimmed **fresh spinach**

3 **eggs**

¼ cup (60 mL) grated **Parmesan cheese**

2 tbsp (30 mL) **all-purpose flour**

1½ tsp (7 mL) **baking powder**

¼ tsp (1 mL) grated **lemon rind**

1 tbsp (15 mL) toasted **sesame seeds,** pine nuts or sliced almonds

LEMON YOGURT SAUCE:

1½ cups (375 mL) **Balkan-style plain yogurt**

⅓ cup (75 mL) thinly sliced **green onions**

1 tbsp (15 mL) **lemon juice**

Pinch each **salt** and **pepper**

✳ These delicate cakes may crumble a bit while being formed but will firm up during frying. Alongside a leafy green salad, serve two cakes for lighter appetites or three for hungrier folks.

GRAINS

In fine sieve, rinse quinoa under cold water; drain. In saucepan, bring quinoa, broth and 1½ cups (375 mL) water to boil. Reduce heat; simmer, covered, for 15 minutes. Drain in fine sieve; let cool completely in sieve.

Meanwhile, in skillet, heat 1 tbsp (15 mL) of the oil over medium heat; fry onion, garlic, salt and pepper, stirring occasionally, until onion is softened, about 4 minutes. Add spinach; cook, stirring, until wilted and no liquid remains, about 3 minutes. Let cool; coarsely chop.

LEMON YOGURT SAUCE: Stir together yogurt, green onions, lemon juice, salt and pepper. Set aside in refrigerator.

In large bowl, whisk eggs, Parmesan cheese, flour, baking powder and lemon rind; fold in quinoa and spinach mixture. With wet hands, form into 16 cakes; transfer to waxed paper–lined tray. Refrigerate for 1 hour.

In nonstick skillet, heat half of the remaining oil over medium-high heat; fry half of the cakes, turning once with 2 spatulas, until golden, about 8 minutes. Keep warm on baking sheet in 200°F (100°C) oven. Repeat with remaining oil and cakes. Serve drizzled with Lemon Yogurt Sauce and sprinkled with sesame seeds.

PER SERVING: about 353 cal, 11 g pro, 22 g total fat (5 g sat. fat), 30 g carb, 3 g fibre, 81 mg chol, 366 mg sodium, 454 mg potassium. % RDI: 17% calcium, 29% iron, 17% vit A, 7% vit C, 24% folate.

Smoked Cheese Risotto

Prep: 10 minutes   **Cook:** 30 minutes   **Makes:** 4 servings

2 cups (500 mL) **vegetable broth**

2 tbsp (30 mL) **butter**

1 tbsp (15 mL) **olive oil**

1 large **shallot** (or half onion), diced

1 clove **garlic,** minced

¼ tsp (1 mL) **salt**

1½ cups (375 mL) **arborio rice**

½ cup (125 mL) **dry white wine**

4 oz (125 g) **smoked cheese** (such as Cheddar, Gouda or provolone), shredded

¼ cup (60 mL) grated **Parmesan cheese** (approx)

2 tbsp (30 mL) minced **fresh chives** or parsley

In small saucepan, bring broth and 2½ cups (625 mL) water to boil; reduce heat to low and keep warm.

In large saucepan, heat 1 tbsp (15 mL) of the butter and oil over medium-high heat; sauté shallot, garlic and salt until shallot is softened but not coloured, about 3 minutes.

Add rice, stirring to coat and toast grains. Add wine; cook, stirring, until almost no liquid remains.

Add 4 cups (1 L) of the broth mixture, ½ cup (125 mL) at a time and stirring after each addition until most of the liquid is absorbed before adding more, about 20 minutes total. Taste before adding last cup. (Rice should be loose, creamy but not mushy, and still slightly firm in centre.)

Add smoked cheese and remaining broth mixture; cook, stirring, until smooth. Remove from heat. Stir in Parmesan cheese and remaining butter. Sprinkle with chives, and more Parmesan if desired.

PER SERVING: about 493 cal, 16 g pro, 19 g total fat (10 g sat. fat), 64 g carb, 1 g fibre, 43 mg chol, 913 mg sodium. % RDI: 27% calcium, 6% iron, 15% vit A, 4% folate.

Spinach & Rice Phyllo Pie

Prep: 20 minutes **Stand:** 10 minutes **Cook:** 1¼ hours **Makes:** 6 servings

¾ cup (175 mL) **parboiled whole-grain brown** or white **rice**

½ tsp (2 mL) **salt**

1½ pkg (each 10 oz/284 g) **fresh spinach,** trimmed

¼ cup (60 mL) **pine nuts**

1 cup (250 mL) **ricotta cheese**

1 cup (250 mL) shredded **old Cheddar cheese**

1 **egg**

1 tbsp (15 mL) finely chopped **fresh dill**

1 tsp (5 mL) grated **lemon rind**

1 tbsp (15 mL) **lemon juice**

¼ tsp (1 mL) **pepper**

Pinch **nutmeg**

6 sheets **phyllo pastry,** thawed

¼ cup (60 mL) **butter,** melted, or olive oil

2 cups (500 mL) **Marinara Sauce** (page 271) or tomato pasta sauce, heated

In saucepan, bring 1½ cups (375 mL) water, rice and salt to boil. Reduce heat; simmer, covered, until tender and no liquid remains, 20 minutes. Remove from heat; let stand for 5 minutes. Transfer to bowl; let cool. Meanwhile, rinse spinach; shake off excess water. In large saucepan, cook spinach, covered, over medium-high heat until wilted, about 3 minutes. Drain and squeeze dry; chop coarsely. Add to cooled rice.

In small dry skillet, toast pine nuts over medium-low heat, stirring often, until golden, about 3 minutes. Add to rice along with ricotta and Cheddar cheeses, egg, dill, lemon rind and juice, pepper and nutmeg; mix well.

Lay 1 sheet phyllo on work surface, covering remainder with damp cloth. Brush with some of the butter; lay in greased 9-inch (23 cm) pie plate, leaving overhang. Repeat with 4 more sheets phyllo, alternating direction of each. Spoon in rice mixture. Brush remaining phyllo with some of the butter; fold in half. Lay over rice mixture; tuck in edges. Bring overhang over top and crumple slightly. Brush top with remaining butter.

Bake in bottom third of 350°F (180°C) oven until golden and crisp, about 45 minutes. Let stand for 5 minutes before slicing. Divide sauce among plates; top each with slice of pie.

PER SERVING: about 494 cal, 19 g pro, 28 g total fat (14 g sat. fat), 44 g carb, 5 g fibre, 96 mg chol, 949 mg sodium. % RDI: 31% calcium, 36% iron, 73% vit A, 23% vit C, 61% folate.

GRAINS

Vegetable Biryani

Prep: 15 minutes   **Cook:** 40 minutes   **Makes:** 4 servings

* This curry-scented vegetable, lentil, dried fruit and nut pilaf is a symphony of textures and flavours. It's great on its own, but you could also serve each plate with a spoonful of plain yogurt or Spinach Raita (page 273). Serve with naan bread if desired.

¾ cup (175 mL) **dried green lentils,** drained and rinsed

2 tbsp (30 mL) **olive oil**

1 **onion,** diced

2 **carrots,** diced

2 cloves **garlic,** minced

1 tbsp (15 mL) **curry paste**

¼ tsp (1 mL) each **salt** and **pepper**

2 cups (500 mL) small **cauliflower florets**

1 cup (250 mL) **basmati rice**

¼ cup (60 mL) **raisins** or dried currants

2¼ cups (550 mL) **vegetable broth**

1 cup (250 mL) frozen **green peas,** thawed

¼ cup (60 mL) toasted **sliced almonds**

In saucepan of boiling water, cook lentils for 10 minutes; drain.

Meanwhile, in Dutch oven, heat oil over medium-high heat; sauté onion until deep golden, about 6 minutes.

Add carrots, garlic, curry paste, salt and pepper; sauté until fragrant, about 3 minutes. Stir in cauliflower, rice, raisins and lentils to coat.

Add broth; bring to boil. Reduce heat and simmer, covered, until rice, lentils and vegetables are tender, about 20 minutes. Stir in peas; cook until heated through, about 4 minutes. Sprinkle with almonds.

PER SERVING: about 503 cal, 18 g pro, 13 g total fat (2 g sat. fat), 82 g carb, 10 g fibre, 0 mg chol, 861 mg sodium. % RDI: 8% calcium, 36% iron, 81% vit A, 47% vit C, 111% folate.

GRAINS

Mushroom Brown Rice Torte

Prep: 20 minutes   **Cook:** 1¾ hours   **Makes:** 8 servings

1 cup (250 mL) **brown rice,** rinsed and drained

2 tbsp (30 mL) **olive oil**

1 **onion,** thinly sliced

1¼ lb (625 g) **mixed mushrooms,** such as cremini, white, oyster or shiitake caps, trimmed and sliced

1 tsp (5 mL) chopped **fresh thyme**

1 tsp (5 mL) **salt**

½ tsp (2 mL) **pepper**

6 **eggs**

3 cups (750 mL) shredded **Fontina** or old Cheddar **cheese**

¾ cup (175 mL) **10% cream** or milk

Line bottom and side of 10-inch (3 L) springform pan with parchment paper; wrap base with foil.

Bring pot of salted water to boil over high heat; stir in rice. Reduce heat and simmer until tender, about 40 minutes. Transfer to fine sieve; let cool completely in sieve.

Meanwhile, in large skillet, heat oil over medium-high heat; sauté onion until softened, about 4 minutes. Add mushrooms, thyme, and half each of the salt and pepper; sauté until mushrooms are softened and liquid is evaporated, 8 to 10 minutes.

Beat 1 of the eggs; stir in rice. Pat evenly into bottom of prepared pan. Sprinkle with half of the cheese; spread mushroom mixture evenly over top.

Beat together remaining eggs, cream and remaining salt and pepper; pour evenly over top. Bake in 400°F (200°C) oven for 45 minutes. Sprinkle with remaining cheese; bake until bubbly and golden, about 15 minutes. Let stand for 15 minutes before cutting into wedges.

PER SERVING: about 372 cal, 20 g pro, 22 g total fat (11 g sat. fat), 24 g carb, 3 g fibre, 192 mg chol, 977 mg sodium, 364 mg potassium. % RDI: 25% calcium, 11% iron, 18% vit A, 2% vit C, 16% folate.

SHIITAKE MUSHROOMS

Fresh or dried, tasty shiitake (pronounced shee-TAH-kay) mushrooms inject a rich earthy flavour into soups, salads, appetizers and main dishes. The third most cultivated mushroom in the world (after white button and oyster), shiitakes have been used for culinary and medicinal purposes by the Chinese for 6,000 years.

TYPES

Fresh: Beige to dark brown, umbrella-shaped shiitakes have long, woody stems and convex 2- to 4-inch (5 to 10 cm) diameter caps, some of which are cracked.

Dried: With a strong, smoky-oak flavour, dried shiitakes must be soaked in warm or boiling water or other liquid prior to using. Make sure to strain and use the soaking liquid – it has tons of flavour. Small packages of dried shiitakes are available in the vegetable section of many grocery stores, but for best value, purchase dried shiitakes in large packages or in bulk in East Asian markets. Of these, Japanese or Chinese winter mushrooms are the best quality and can be identified by their thick, cracked, pale tops.

HOW TO CHOOSE, STORE AND USE

• Choose fresh shiitakes with plump, firm tops and no trace of wetness or mildew.
• Place in paper bag, or unwrap plastic-sealed container and cover with damp paper towel. Refrigerate for up to 1 week.
• With scissors or knife, remove woody stems (though too tough to eat, stems add great flavour to stocks). Wipe caps with damp towel; do not rinse because they are porous and will absorb water.

Roasted Cauliflower Risotto

Prep: 10 minutes   **Cook:** 45 minutes   **Makes:** 4 servings

1 head **cauliflower** (about 2 lb/1 kg)

3 cloves **garlic**

3 tbsp (45 mL) **extra-virgin olive oil**

½ tsp (2 mL) **salt**

1¼ cups (300 mL) **vegetable broth**

1 large **shallot** (or half onion), minced

1 cup (250 mL) **arborio rice**

¼ cup (60 mL) **dry white wine**

⅓ cup (75 mL) grated **Parmesan cheese**

2 tbsp (30 mL) chopped **fresh parsley**

* Roasting cauliflower florets and garlic cloves caramelizes them and further brings out their natural sweetness.

Trim cauliflower; cut into florets. Toss together with garlic, 2 tbsp (30 mL) of the oil and ¼ tsp (1 mL) of the salt. Roast on greased baking sheet in 400°F (200°C) oven until golden and tender, 35 to 45 minutes. Mash garlic with fork.

Meanwhile, in small saucepan, bring broth and 1¾ cups (425 mL) water to boil; reduce heat to low and keep warm.

In large saucepan, heat remaining oil over medium-high heat; fry shallot and remaining salt, stirring occasionally, until softened but not coloured, about 3 minutes.

Add rice, stirring to coat and toast grains. Add wine; cook, stirring, until almost no liquid remains, about 1 minute.

Add broth mixture, ½ cup (125 mL) at a time and stirring after each addition until most of the liquid is absorbed before adding more, 18 to 20 minutes total. (Rice should be loose, creamy but not mushy, and still slightly firm in centre of kernel.)

Stir in cauliflower, garlic, cheese and parsley.

PER SERVING: about 351 cal, 10 g pro, 13 g total fat (3 g sat. fat), 49 g carb, 5 g fibre, 9 mg chol, 678 mg sodium, 297 mg potassium. % RDI: 12% calcium, 9% iron, 6% vit A, 112% vit C, 32% folate.

Mushroom Maki Rolls

Prep: 20 minutes **Stand:** 15 minutes **Cook:** 7 minutes **Makes:** 48 pieces

✳ Serve with pickled sushi ginger and, if available, sushi soy sauce, which is milder and sweeter than regular soy sauce. You can replace the watercress with baby arugula if you prefer.

1¼ lb (625 g) **shiitake mushroom caps**

2 tsp (10 mL) **vegetable oil**

2 tsp (10 mL) **sesame oil**

2 cloves **garlic,** minced

1 tbsp (15 mL) **mirin** (Japanese sweet rice wine) or sherry

1 tbsp (15 mL) **sodium-reduced soy sauce** or sushi soy sauce

1 pkg (3½ oz/100 g) **enoki** or beech **mushrooms**

6 sheets **roasted nori**

Sushi Rice (opposite)

3 **green onions,** thinly sliced lengthwise

1 cup (250 mL) trimmed **watercress**

Halve shiitake caps if large. In skillet, heat vegetable and sesame oils over medium-high heat; sauté shiitakes and garlic until softened, about 5 minutes.

Stir in mirin and soy sauce; cook until liquid is evaporated, about 2 minutes. Scrape into bowl; let cool for 15 minutes.

Trim roots off enoki mushrooms; separate enokis into strands.

Place 1 nori sheet, shiny side down and with long side closest, on bamboo sushi rolling mat. With moistened fingers, lightly spread about ½ cup (125 mL) of the rice over nori in even layer, leaving ½-inch (1 cm) border along each long side.

Lay one-sixth of the shiitake mixture in horizontal line about 2 inches (5 cm) in from closest long edge; lay one-sixth of the enoki mushrooms on top. Top with one-sixth each of the green onions and watercress.

Using bamboo mat to lift and starting with closest long edge, roll up nori, firmly encasing filling. Set aside, seam side down. Repeat with remaining ingredients to make 6 rolls. (To hold, wrap each in paper towel and set aside for up to 2 hours at room temperature.)

Trim ends even. Cut each roll into 8 slices, wiping knife with wet cloth between cuts.

PER PIECE: about 23 cal, 1 g pro, trace total fat (0 g sat. fat), 4 g carb, trace fibre, 0 mg chol, 52 mg sodium. % RDI: 1% iron, 1% vit A, 2% vit C, 2% folate.

SUSHI RICE

Prep: 5 minutes   **Stand:** 40 minutes   **Cook:** 15 minutes
Makes: about 3 cups (750 mL)

1 cup (250 mL) **medium-grain sushi rice**

3 tbsp (45 mL) **unseasoned rice vinegar**

4 tsp (20 mL) **granulated sugar**

¾ tsp (4 mL) **salt**

In fine sieve, rinse rice in 4 changes of cold water, stirring vigorously until water runs clear. Drain well.

In saucepan, bring rice and 1¼ cups (300 mL) water to boil over high heat; stir once. Reduce heat and simmer, covered, for 13 minutes. Remove from heat. Uncover and drape tea towel over top; replace lid, letting edges of towel hang over side. Let stand for 10 minutes. Transfer to large glass baking dish or bowl.

Meanwhile, microwave rice vinegar, sugar and salt at high until hot, about 25 seconds. Stir just until sugar is dissolved; let cool completely.

Drizzle over rice; gently toss with wooden spoon to coat grains. To cool rice quickly, spread over surface of baking dish; loosely cover with tea towel and let cool completely at room temperature, about 30 minutes. Do not refrigerate.

PER 1 TBSP (15 mL): about 16 cal, trace pro, 0 g total fat (0 g sat. fat), 3 g carb, trace fibre, 0 mg chol, 37 mg sodium.

GRAINS

GRAINS

GREAT GRAINS

WHEAT

Wheat berries: Whole unmilled kernels of hard or soft wheat. Interchangeable in recipes, soft wheat berries take about 15 minutes less cooking time than the more-available hard berries.

Bulgur: Whole wheat berries steamed and hulled then dried and cracked. Bulgur is graded according to size into fine, medium or coarse categories, which are usually interchangeable in recipes.

Couscous: Cracked durum or semolina wheat that's steamed then dried. North African– or Moroccan-type couscous is a small granular pastalike grain that's great served with stews or curries, or used as a salad or stuffing base.

Israeli couscous: Small white peppercorn-size toasted semolina pasta; sometimes called pearl couscous or *maftoul*. Israeli couscous is a nice alternative to rice in risottos or sweet puddings.

Barley: Believed to be the oldest cultivated grain, barley most commonly appears in its hulled and polished form, called pearl barley. Pot barley is the whole grain with bran intact; it takes longer to cook than pearl barley. Barley flakes are processed like rolled oats.

Cornmeal: Made from ground white or yellow (or sometimes blue) corn, cornmeal is available in coarse, medium or fine grinds. Generally, coarse cornmeal is used for polenta, while the finer grinds are used for baking. This grain is gluten-free.

Millet: Small and round, this mild-tasting, gluten-free grain is used in baked goods, breads and pilafs or as a base for stews, curries and stuffings.

Rye: Similar in shape to and slightly darker than wheat kernels, rye kernels can be ground into flour for baking or processed like rolled oats for cereals or baking. Left whole, they can be used in the same ways as wheat berries but require less cooking time.

Spelt: One of the most cultivated of the ancient grains, spelt grains look like wheat grains but are slightly smaller. Spelt flour can be used in baking, and whole hulled grains can be cooked like rice for salads or in soups.

OATS

Steel-cut oats: Hulled oat kernels that are cut into two or three pieces. They're also called Irish or Scottish oats.

Rolled oats: Hulled oat kernels that are steamed then rolled. Quick-cooking oats are made by increasing the heat during the steaming process.

Quinoa Dolmades with Tahini Yogurt Sauce

Prep: 30 minutes   **Stand:** 15 minutes   **Cook:** 1½ hours   **Makes:** 36 pieces

* Quinoa takes the place of more-traditional rice in this Greek and Turkish finger food. Grape leaves are available at Middle Eastern, Greek and Italian grocery stores and most supermarkets.

36 drained **bottled grape leaves**
1 cup (250 mL) **quinoa**
1 tbsp (15 mL) **olive oil**
1 **onion,** diced
1 tsp (5 mL) **ground cumin**
½ tsp (2 mL) **ground coriander**
¼ tsp (1 mL) **cinnamon**
¼ tsp (1 mL) each **salt** and **pepper**

⅓ cup (75 mL) **dried currants**
⅓ cup (75 mL) chopped **Kalamata olives**
⅓ cup (75 mL) toasted **pine nuts**
¼ cup (60 mL) chopped **fresh mint**
1¼ cups (300 mL) **vegetable broth**
1 tbsp (15 mL) **lemon juice**
Tahini Yogurt Sauce (opposite)

In large heatproof bowl, cover grape leaves with boiling water; let stand for 5 minutes. Drain well; let cool.

In fine sieve, rinse quinoa under cold running water; drain. In saucepan, heat oil over medium heat; fry onion, stirring occasionally, until softened, about 5 minutes.

Stir in cumin, coriander, cinnamon, salt and pepper; cook for 1 minute. Add quinoa, currants and olives; cook, stirring, until quinoa is toasted, about 2 minutes.

Stir in 2 cups (500 mL) water; bring to boil. Reduce heat and simmer, covered, until liquid is evaporated and quinoa is tender, 15 to 20 minutes. Let cool. Stir in pine nuts and mint.

Remove tough stems from grape leaves. Lay leaves, vein side up, on work surface. Place 1 tbsp (15 mL) filling in centre of each; fold in sides and roll snugly into cigar shapes.

Place dolmades, seam side down, in single layer in 13- x 9-inch (3 L) glass baking dish. Combine broth with lemon juice; pour over top. Cover tightly with foil; bake in 350°F (180°C) oven until liquid is evaporated, about 1 hour. Let cool for 20 minutes.

Serve warm, at room temperature or chilled, with Tahini Yogurt Sauce for dipping.

PER PIECE: about 61 cal, 2 g pro, 4 g total fat (1 g sat. fat), 6 g carb, 1 g fibre, 1 mg chol, 205 mg sodium, 82 mg potassium. % RDI: 3% calcium, 6% iron, 1% vit A, 2% vit C, 4% folate.

TAHINI YOGURT SAUCE

Prep: 5 minutes   **Makes:** about 1⅓ cups (325 mL)

1 cup (250 mL) **Balkan-style plain yogurt**

¼ cup (60 mL) **tahini**

2 tbsp (30 mL) chopped **fresh parsley**

2 tbsp (30 mL) **warm water**

1 tbsp (15 mL) **extra-virgin olive oil**

2 tsp (10 mL) **lemon juice**

¼ tsp (1 mL) each **salt** and **pepper**

Whisk together yogurt, tahini, parsley, water, oil, lemon juice, salt and pepper until smooth.

PER 1 TBSP (15 mL): about 34 cal, 1 g pro, 3 g total fat (1 g sat. fat), 2 g carb, trace fibre, 2 mg chol, 37 mg sodium, 38 mg potassium. % RDI: 3% calcium, 2% iron, 1% vit A, 2% vit C, 2% folate.

GRAINS

Sushi Vegetable Pizza

Prep: 30 minutes   **Stand:** 1¼ hours   **Cook:** 45 minutes   **Makes:** 4 servings

✳ Don't be fooled by the lightweight appearance of these beautiful sushi squares – they're filling.

8 **dried shiitake mushrooms** (1 oz/30 g)

¼ cup (60 mL) **sodium-reduced soy sauce**

2 tbsp (30 mL) **unseasoned rice vinegar**

1½ tbsp (22 mL) **granulated sugar**

½ cup (125 mL) **light mayonnaise**

1½ tsp (7 mL) **wasabi paste**

2 sheets **roasted nori**

Quarter **English cucumber,** halved lengthwise and thinly sliced crosswise

1 **avocado,** peeled, pitted and thinly sliced

2 tbsp (30 mL) drained **pickled sushi ginger**

RICE:

1 cup (250 mL) **medium-grain sushi rice**

2 tbsp (30 mL) **unseasoned rice vinegar**

1 tbsp (15 mL) **granulated sugar**

¾ tsp (4 mL) **salt**

2 tsp (10 mL) **vegetable oil** (approx)

½ cup (125 mL) **panko** (Japanese dry bread crumbs)

Stir together mushrooms, soy sauce, vinegar, sugar and ⅓ cup (75 mL) water; microwave at high until hot, about 45 seconds. Stir to coat mushrooms; let stand for 5 minutes. Reserving soy mixture, squeeze liquid from mushrooms; trim off and discard stems. Thinly slice mushrooms; return to soy mixture. Microwave at high for 30 seconds.

RICE: In fine sieve, rinse rice in 4 changes of cold water, stirring vigorously until water runs clear. Drain well. In saucepan, bring rice and 1¼ cups (300 mL) water to boil; stir. Reduce heat and simmer, covered and without stirring, until rice is tender and no liquid remains, about 25 minutes.

Meanwhile, stir together vinegar, sugar and salt; microwave at high until hot, about 25 seconds. Stir until sugar dissolves. Drizzle over rice; gently toss with wooden spoon to coat grains. Spread evenly in greased 8-inch (2 L) square cake pan; let cool completely, about 1 hour.

Lightly brush top of rice with oil; sprinkle with half of the panko, pressing lightly to adhere. Place remaining panko in shallow dish. With greased knife, cut rice into 4 squares. With large metal spatula, carefully lift out and place each square on panko, pressing lightly to coat bottom. Transfer to greased parchment paper– or foil-lined baking sheet. Bake in 425°F (220°C) oven until crust is crisp and panko is golden, 15 to 20 minutes.

Meanwhile, mix together mayonnaise, wasabi and 2 tsp (10 mL) water. Dip nori sheets in cold water to dampen; pat dry. Thinly slice into strips.

Drain mushrooms. Top each rice patty with mushrooms, cucumber, then fanned slices of avocado. Drizzle with wasabi cream; top with nori and ginger (or serve ginger on the side).

PER SERVING: about 454 cal, 7 g pro, 20 g total fat (3 g sat. fat), 64 g carb, 6 g fibre, 10 mg chol, 1,189 mg sodium, 458 mg potassium. % RDI: 3% calcium, 13% iron, 5% vit A, 15% vit C, 29% folate.

[PASTA

Tagliatelle with Parmesan,
Pine Nuts & Lemon
(page 90)

Chilled Asian Noodle Salad

Prep: 25 minutes   **Stand:** 15 minutes   **Cook:** 8 minutes   **Makes:** 4 servings

8 **dried shiitake mushrooms**
(1 oz/30 g)

½ cup (125 mL) **boiling water**

¼ cup (60 mL) **tahini**

¼ cup (60 mL) **sodium-reduced
soy sauce**

¼ cup (60 mL) **sesame oil**

¼ cup (60 mL) **vegetable oil**

3 tbsp (45 mL) **unseasoned
rice vinegar**

2 tsp (10 mL) grated **fresh ginger**

1 tsp (5 mL) **granulated sugar**

¼ tsp (1 mL) **Asian hot sauce** (such
as sriracha) or hot pepper sauce

8 oz (250 g) **spaghetti** or soba
noodles

2 cups (500 mL) shredded **napa
cabbage**

1 cup (250 mL) grated **carrot**

1 cup (250 mL) **snow peas,** thinly
sliced lengthwise on diagonal

1 **green onion,** thinly sliced

¼ cup (60 mL) chopped **fresh
coriander**

¼ cup (60 mL) chopped **roasted
peanuts**

Break stems off shiitake mushrooms; soak mushrooms in boiling water
until softened, about 15 minutes. Reserving soaking liquid, squeeze
mushrooms dry; slice. Place in large bowl.

Whisk together ¼ cup (60 mL) of the reserved soaking liquid, tahini, soy
sauce, sesame and vegetable oils, vinegar, ginger, sugar and hot sauce.

Meanwhile, in large pot of boiling salted water, cook spaghetti until
al dente, about 8 minutes. Drain and chill under cold water; drain well.
Add to mushrooms.

Add soy sauce mixture, cabbage, carrot, snow peas, green onion,
coriander and peanuts; toss to coat.

PER SERVING: about 670 cal, 15 g pro, 37 g total fat (4 g sat. fat), 76 g carb, 9 g
fibre, 0 mg chol, 847 mg sodium. % RDI: 8% calcium, 32% iron, 83% vit A, 45% vit C,
96% folate.

Soba Noodles with Pea Shoots & Shiitakes

Prep: 10 minutes   **Cook:** 15 minutes   **Makes:** 6 servings

✳ Sriracha is a smooth and zingy chili sauce from Thailand, while sambal oelek, from Indonesia, is a bit thicker and more like a chili paste. Both are available in Asian markets and many grocery stores. No pea shoots? Replace with thinly sliced bok choy.

8 oz/250 g **soba noodles**

1 tbsp (15 mL) **sesame oil**

1 tbsp (15 mL) **vegetable oil**

2 cloves **garlic,** minced

10 oz (300 g) **shiitake mushrooms,** stemmed and sliced

12 oz (375 g) **snow pea shoots** (about 8 cups/2 L)

⅓ cup (75 mL) **light mayonnaise**

¼ cup (60 mL) **sodium-reduced soy sauce**

1 tbsp (15 mL) **unseasoned rice vinegar**

1 tsp (5 mL) **granulated sugar**

1 tsp (5 mL) **sambal oelek,** sriracha or hot sauce

In large pot of boiling water, cook soba noodles, stirring gently, until tender, about 5 minutes. Drain and chill under cold water; drain well. Transfer to large bowl.

In wok or large skillet, heat half each of the sesame and vegetable oils over medium-high heat; sauté garlic until fragrant, about 15 seconds.

Add mushrooms; sauté until tender, about 4 minutes. Add to noodles.

In wok, heat remaining oils; stir-fry pea shoots until wilted and tender, about 5 minutes. Add to noodle mixture.

Whisk together mayonnaise, soy sauce, rice vinegar, sugar and sambal oelek; toss with noodle mixture to coat. Serve at room temperature or chilled.

PER SERVING: about 247 cal, 10 g pro, 10 g total fat (1 g sat. fat), 34 g carb, 4 g fibre, 5 mg chol, 523 mg sodium, 186 mg potassium. % RDI: 1% calcium, 8% iron, 21% vit A, 47% vit C, 18% folate.

ASIAN NOODLES

Buckwheat noodles (*soba*): Thin, flat Japanese noodles, soba noodles are made from buckwheat and wheat flours. Because of the low-gluten buckwheat, they puff up as they cook until they're almost round. Recipes calling for buckwheat noodles can also be made with **chasoba,** thin green noodles flavoured with green tea powder.

Substitute: Japanese thin wheat noodles (**somen**), vermicelli pasta or thin spinach linguine

Rice noodles (rice sticks, rice vermicelli): Made from rice flour, these are popular southern Chinese and southeast Asian noodles. Rice sticks, which come in varying widths, are used in soups and stir-fries and are featured in many cold noodle dishes, especially in Vietnam. For cold noodle dishes, the best choices are the medium and thin widths, as well as the thinnest, rice vermicelli. They are generally available at grocery stores but you can find an even larger variety at Asian food stores.

Substitute: Spaghettini or thin linguine

Wheat noodles: Vastly popular throughout China and Japan, wheat noodles are made of hard wheat flour and water, like pasta. Chinese and Japanese wheat noodles (called **chuka soba** or **ramen**) are white and most often flat.

Substitute: Any long pasta, such as fettuccine, linguine, spaghettini or spaghetti

Japanese Noodle Salad

Prep: 15 minutes   **Stand:** 15 minutes   **Cook:** 8 minutes   **Makes:** 4 servings

1 pkg (340 g) **instant chuka soba noodles** or ramen

2 **eggs**

1 **green onion** (green part only)

1 tsp (5 mL) **vegetable oil**

1 cup (250 mL) shredded **lettuce**

Half **English cucumber,** julienned

2 **plum tomatoes,** quartered

1 tbsp (15 mL) toasted **sesame seeds**

DRESSING:

8 **dried shiitake mushrooms** (1 oz/30 g)

1 cup (250 mL) **boiling water**

3 tbsp (45 mL) **unseasoned rice vinegar**

2 tbsp (30 mL) **soy sauce**

4 tsp (20 mL) **granulated sugar**

1 tsp (5 mL) **sesame oil**

DRESSING: Break off shiitake mushroom stems; soak mushrooms in boiling water until softened, about 15 minutes. Reserving soaking liquid, remove mushrooms and squeeze dry; thinly slice. Strain soaking liquid into small bowl; stir in vinegar, soy sauce, sugar and sesame oil.

Meanwhile, cook noodles according to package directions. Drain and chill under cold water; drain well.

Beat eggs with 1 tsp (5 mL) water; stir in green onion. In nonstick skillet, heat oil over medium-low heat; cook egg mixture, covered and without stirring, to make thin omelette, about 3 minutes. Slice thinly.

Divide noodles among 4 plates. Surround with piles of lettuce, cucumber, tomatoes, omelette strips and mushrooms; sprinkle with sesame seeds. Serve with 4 small dishes of Dressing to pour over top.

PER SERVING: about 465 cal, 22 g pro, 6 g total fat (1 g sat. fat), 90 g carb, 8 g fibre, 93 mg chol, 953 mg sodium. % RDI: 5% calcium, 21% iron, 7% vit A, 11% vit C, 42% folate.

Tagliatelle with Parmesan, Pine Nuts & Lemon

Prep: 5 minutes **Stand:** 30 minutes **Cook:** 10 minutes **Makes:** 4 servings

⅓ cup (75 mL) **pine nuts**

⅓ cup (75 mL) minced **fresh parsley**

3 tbsp (45 mL) **extra-virgin olive oil**

1 tbsp (15 mL) finely grated **lemon rind**

2 tbsp (30 mL) **lemon juice**

¼ tsp (1 mL) each **salt** and **pepper**

12 oz (375 g) **tagliatelle** or fettuccine

¾ cup (175 mL) grated **Parmigiano-Reggiano** or Parmesan **cheese**

In small skillet, toast pine nuts over medium-low heat, stirring often, until light golden, about 3 minutes. Let cool.

Stir together ¼ cup (60 mL) of the parsley, oil, lemon rind and juice, salt and pepper; let stand, covered, for 30 minutes.

Meanwhile, in large pot of boiling salted water, cook pasta until al dente, about 8 minutes. Reserving ¾ cup (175 mL) of the cooking water, drain; return pasta to pot. Toss with lemon mixture, reserved cooking liquid, cheese and half of the pine nuts.

Transfer to large bowl or platter; sprinkle with remaining parsley and pine nuts.

PASTA

PER SERVING: about 567 cal, 20 g pro, 25 g total fat (5 g sat. fat), 67 g carb, 5 g fibre, 17 mg chol, 657 mg sodium. % RDI: 21% calcium, 31% iron, 6% vit A, 22% vit C, 85% folate.

PASTA POINTERS

• Pasta should move while it cooks so it doesn't stick together. Allow about 4 cups (1 L) water for every 4 oz (125 g) pasta. Stir often until water returns to boil that's hard enough to move pasta around freely.

• Add salt to water. This seasons the pasta as it cooks.

• Cooking time begins when pasta and water return to boil.

• Cook pasta until al dente, or tender but still firm. To test, remove a piece and taste.

• Drain pasta very well (you may want to reserve some of the cooking water to add to your pasta sauce).

• Have sauce almost ready before cooking pasta. Most hot pasta dishes do not wait well.

• To replace dried pasta with fresh, use about one-and-a-half times the quantity called for, cooking for 1 to 3 minutes.

PASTA

Crunchy Baked Macaroni & Cheese

Prep: 10 minutes   **Cook:** 40 minutes   **Makes:** 4 to 6 servings

¼ cup (60 mL) **butter**
Half **onion,** diced
½ tsp (2 mL) **salt**
Pinch **cayenne pepper**
2 tbsp (30 mL) **all-purpose flour**
2 cups (500 mL) **milk**
2 tsp (10 mL) **Dijon mustard**

2 cups (500 mL) shredded **old Cheddar cheese**
2 cups (500 mL) **macaroni**
1 cup (250 mL) **panko** (Japanese dry bread crumbs) or fresh bread crumbs

In large saucepan, melt half of the butter over medium heat; fry onion, salt and cayenne pepper, stirring occasionally, until onion is softened, about 5 minutes.

Stir in flour; cook, stirring, for 2 minutes. Whisk in milk and mustard; cook, whisking, until bubbly and thickened, about 5 minutes. Remove from heat; in 2 additions, stir in 1½ cups (375 mL) of the cheese until smooth.

Meanwhile, in large pot of boiling salted water, cook pasta until al dente, about 8 minutes. Drain. Add to sauce; toss to coat. Scrape into greased 6- or 8-cup (1.5 or 2 L) casserole dish.

Melt remaining butter; toss together with panko and remaining cheese. Sprinkle over macaroni mixture. Bake in 375°F (190°C) oven until bubbly and golden, about 25 minutes.

PER EACH OF 6 SERVINGS: about 421 cal, 17 g pro, 23 g total fat (14 g sat. fat), 37 g carb, 2 g fibre, 66 mg chol, 634 mg sodium, 210 mg potassium. % RDI: 35% calcium, 14% iron, 21% vit A, 40% folate.

Spaghettini with Homemade Ricotta & Herbs

Prep: 5 minutes **Cook:** 8 minutes **Makes:** 4 servings

* While store-bought ricotta is fine, this is a dish of sheer beauty and simplicity when using freshly made ricotta. To make fresh bread crumbs, finely chop crustless day-old bread in a food processor until in crumbs.

PASTA

12 oz (375 g) **spaghettini**

2 tbsp (30 mL) **butter**

¾ cup (175 mL) **fresh bread crumbs**

2 cups (500 mL) **Homemade Ricotta** (page 258)

¼ cup (60 mL) chopped **fresh basil**

In large pot of boiling salted water, cook pasta until al dente, about 8 minutes. Reserving 1 cup (250 mL) of the cooking water, drain; return pasta to pot.

Meanwhile, in skillet, melt butter over medium-high heat; sauté bread crumbs, stirring often, until crisp and golden, about 3 minutes. Remove from heat.

Add ricotta, basil and ½ cup (125 mL) of the reserved cooking water to pasta; toss to coat, adding more of the reserved cooking water if desired.

Transfer to serving dish; sprinkle with 2 tbsp (30 mL) of the bread crumbs. Serve with remaining crumbs to sprinkle over top.

PER SERVING: about 589 cal, 24 g pro, 23 g total fat (13 g sat. fat), 71 g carb, 4 g fibre, 74 mg chol, 511 mg sodium, 237 mg potassium. % RDI: 40% calcium, 25% iron, 18% vit A, 3% vit C, 90% folate.

Spaghetti with Roasted Cherry Tomato Sauce & Basil

Prep: 15 minutes   **Cook:** 25 minutes   **Makes:** 4 servings

12 oz (375 g) **spaghetti**

¼ cup (60 mL) thinly sliced **fresh basil**

¼ cup (60 mL) crumbled **goat cheese**

¼ cup (60 mL) sliced **black olives**

ROASTED CHERRY TOMATO SAUCE:

4 cups (1 L) **cherry tomatoes,** halved

4 cloves **garlic,** sliced

3 tbsp (45 mL) **extra-virgin olive oil**

1 tbsp (15 mL) **balsamic vinegar**

2 tsp (10 mL) minced **fresh rosemary**

½ tsp (2 mL) **salt**

Pinch **hot pepper flakes**

ROASTED CHERRY TOMATO SAUCE: In 13- x 9-inch (3 L) glass baking dish, toss together tomatoes, garlic, oil, vinegar, rosemary, salt and hot pepper flakes. Roast in 400°F (200°C) oven until shrivelled, about 25 minutes.

Meanwhile, in large pot of boiling salted water, cook pasta until al dente, about 8 minutes. Drain; transfer to large serving bowl.

Toss with Roasted Cherry Tomato Sauce and basil to coat. Sprinkle with goat cheese and olives.

PASTA

PER SERVING: about 474 cal, 14 g pro, 15 g total fat (3 g sat. fat), 72 g carb, 6 g fibre, 4 mg chol, 620 mg sodium. % RDI: 6% calcium, 30% iron, 16% vit A, 32% vit C, 87% folate.

Spaghetti with Roasted Cherry
Tomato Sauce & Basil
(page 95)

Ricotta & Feta Shells

Prep: 20 minutes   **Cook:** 1¼ hours   **Makes:** 6 to 8 servings

24 jumbo **pasta shells**

FILLING:

1 tub (454 g) **ricotta cheese**

1 cup (250 mL) crumbled **feta cheese**

2 **eggs**

2 tsp (10 mL) **dried oregano**

¾ tsp (4 mL) grated **lemon rind**

½ tsp (2 mL) **pepper**

¼ cup (60 mL) thinly sliced **green onions**

SAUCE:

1 tbsp (15 mL) **extra-virgin olive oil**

1 **onion**, chopped

2 cloves **garlic**, minced

¾ tsp (4 mL) **dried oregano**

¼ tsp (1 mL) each **salt** and **pepper**

1 can (28 oz/796 mL) **crushed tomatoes**

1 cup (250 mL) chopped drained bottled **roasted red peppers**

¼ cup (60 mL) chopped **fresh parsley**

SAUCE: In large saucepan, heat oil over medium heat; fry onion, garlic, oregano, salt and pepper, stirring occasionally, until onion is softened, about 5 minutes.

Add tomatoes and red peppers; bring to boil. Reduce heat and simmer until thickened, about 20 minutes. Stir in parsley.

FILLING: Meanwhile, mix together ricotta, feta, eggs, oregano, lemon rind and pepper; stir in green onions.

In large saucepan of boiling salted water, cook pasta until al dente, about 10 minutes. Drain and chill under cold water; drain well.

Spread 2 cups (500 mL) of the Sauce in 13- x 9-inch (3 L) glass baking dish. Spoon heaping 1 tbsp (15 mL) of the Filling into each pasta shell. Arrange, stuffed side up, over sauce; spoon remaining sauce over top. (If not baking right away, cover and refrigerate for up to 24 hours; add 10 minutes to baking time.)

Bake in 350°F (180°C) oven until bubbly, about 40 minutes.

PER EACH OF 8 SERVINGS: about 393 cal, 19 g pro, 16 g total fat (9 g sat. fat), 46 g carb, 5 g fibre, 94 mg chol, 545 mg sodium. % RDI: 26% calcium, 29% iron, 29% vit A, 87% vit C, 57% folate.

Eggplant & Spinach Lasagna

Prep: 1 hour   **Stand:** 40 minutes   **Cook:** 1¾ hours   **Makes:** 8 servings

2 large **eggplants** (about 2½ lb/1.25 kg total)

1 tsp (5 mL) **salt**

12 **lasagna noodles**

3 tbsp (45 mL) **extra-virgin olive oil**

3 bags (each 10 oz/284 g) **fresh spinach,** trimmed

½ cup (125 mL) toasted **pine nuts**

3 **eggs,** lightly beaten

3 cups (750 mL) **ricotta cheese**

3 cups (750 mL) shredded **mozzarella cheese** (10 oz/300 g)

1½ cups (375 mL) grated **Romano** or Parmesan **cheese**

½ tsp (2 mL) **pepper**

½ tsp (2 mL) **nutmeg**

TOMATO SAUCE:

1 tbsp (15 mL) **extra-virgin olive oil**

1 **onion,** finely chopped

2 cloves **garlic,** minced

¼ tsp (1 mL) **hot pepper flakes**

1 can (28 oz/796 mL) **whole tomatoes**

2 tsp (10 mL) **dried oregano**

Peel eggplants; cut lengthwise into ¼-inch (5 mm) thick slices. Sprinkle both sides with salt. Layer in colander; let stand for 30 minutes.

TOMATO SAUCE: Meanwhile, in saucepan, heat oil over medium heat; fry onion, garlic and hot pepper flakes, stirring, until onion is softened, 2 minutes. Add tomatoes and oregano, breaking up with spoon; bring to boil. Reduce heat and simmer until slightly thickened, 20 minutes.

Meanwhile, in large pot of boiling salted water, cook pasta until al dente, 8 to 10 minutes. Drain and chill under cold water; drain. Arrange in single layer between damp towels.

Press eggplant slices firmly to remove liquid. Transfer to paper towels; let dry. Brush with 2 tbsp (30 mL) of the oil; place in single layer on parchment paper–lined baking sheets. Bake in 450°F (230°C) oven, turning once, until lightly browned, 20 to 25 minutes.

Meanwhile, rinse spinach; shake off excess water. In large pot, cook spinach, in batches, over medium-high heat, stirring once, until wilted, about 5 minutes. Drain; squeeze out moisture. Chop coarsely. Mix spinach with remaining oil and pine nuts.

Mix together eggs, ricotta, 2 cups (500 mL) of the mozzarella, 1¼ cups (300 mL) of the Romano cheese, pepper and nutmeg.

Spread half of the Tomato Sauce in 13- x 9-inch (3 L) glass baking dish. Top with one-third of the noodles in single layer, half of the spinach mixture, half of the cheese mixture, and half of the eggplant slices, overlapping if necessary; repeat noodle, spinach, cheese and eggplant layers once. Top with remaining noodles and tomato sauce. Sprinkle with remaining mozzarella and Romano cheeses. (If not baking right away, let cool for 30 minutes; cover and refrigerate for up to 12 hours. Add 10 minutes to covered baking time.)

Cover loosely with foil; bake in 375°F (190°C) oven for 25 minutes. Uncover and bake until bubbly and cheese is lightly browned, about 30 minutes. Let stand for 10 minutes before serving.

PER SERVING: about 716 cal, 39 g pro, 44 g total fat (20 g sat. fat), 46 g carb, 9 g fibre, 177 mg chol, 917 mg sodium. % RDI: 78% calcium, 48% iron, 121% vit A, 37% vit C, 110% folate.

Penne with Green Beans, Potatoes & Pesto

Prep: 15 minutes   **Cook:** 15 minutes   **Makes:** 4 servings

8 oz (250 g) **green beans,** halved
   crosswise

10 oz (300 g) **penne rigate**

10 oz (300 g) **mini red-skinned
   potatoes,** scrubbed and
   quartered

PESTO:
¼ cup (60 mL) toasted **pine nuts**

¼ cup (60 mL) grated **Parmesan
   cheese**

2 cloves **garlic,** minced

1 cup (250 mL) packed **fresh basil
   leaves**

¼ cup (60 mL) **extra-virgin olive
   oil**

¼ tsp (1 mL) **salt**

Pinch **pepper**

In large pot of boiling salted water, cook green beans until tender-crisp, about 4 minutes. With slotted spoon, transfer to bowl; let cool.

In same pot, cook pasta until al dente, about 10 minutes. Reserving ½ cup (125 mL) of the cooking water, drain; return pasta to pot.

Meanwhile, in separate saucepan of boiling salted water, cover and cook potatoes until tender, about 10 minutes. Drain well.

PESTO: Meanwhile, in food processor, pulse together pine nuts, Parmesan cheese and garlic until smooth. Add basil, oil, salt and pepper; pulse until smooth.

Add Pesto, green beans, potatoes and reserved cooking water to pasta; toss to coat.

PER SERVING: about 534 cal, 15 g pro, 22 g total fat (3 g sat. fat), 70 g carb, 7 g fibre, 4 mg chol, 731 mg sodium, 533 mg potassium. % RDI: 12% calcium, 31% iron, 10% vit A, 30% vit C, 82% folate.

Artichoke Pesto Linguine

Prep: 5 minutes   **Cook:** 8 minutes   **Makes:** 4 servings

* Since you only need half of the pesto for this dish, you can refrigerate the leftovers for another recipe. Or make a double batch of linguine.

12 oz (375 g) **linguine**

2 jars (each 6 oz/170 mL) **marinated artichokes,** drained and rinsed

½ cup (125 mL) coarsely chopped **fresh parsley**

¼ cup (60 mL) toasted **pine nuts**

¼ cup (60 mL) grated **Parmesan cheese**

¼ cup (60 mL) **extra-virgin olive oil**

¼ tsp (1 mL) each **salt** and **pepper**

In large pot of boiling salted water, cook pasta until al dente, about 8 minutes. Reserving ¾ cup (175 mL) of the cooking water, drain; return pasta to pot or transfer to serving bowl.

Meanwhile, in food processor, pulse together artichokes, parsley, pine nuts, Parmesan cheese, oil, salt and pepper until smooth. Transfer half to small airtight container and refrigerate for up to 3 days (or freeze for up to 2 weeks).

Add remaining pesto to pasta along with enough of the reserved cooking water to moisten; toss to coat.

PER SERVING: about 454 cal, 14 g pro, 14 g total fat (2 g sat. fat), 68 g carb, 6 g fibre, 3 mg chol, 445 mg sodium. % RDI: 6% calcium, 29% iron, 4% vit A, 12% vit C, 88% folate.

Pasta with Mushroom Bolognese

Prep: 12 minutes   **Cook:** 40 minutes   **Makes:** 4 servings

2 tbsp (30 mL) **olive oil**

1 **onion,** chopped

4 cloves **garlic,** minced

1 **carrot,** diced

1 stalk **celery,** diced

8 cups (2 L) finely chopped cremini or white **mushrooms** (1½ lb/750 g)

1 cup (250 mL) **vegetable broth**

½ tsp (2 mL) each **salt** and **pepper**

Pinch **nutmeg**

1 **bay leaf**

1 can (28 oz/796 mL) **diced tomatoes**

¼ cup (60 mL) **tomato paste**

12 oz (375 g) **bucatini** or spaghetti

½ cup (125 mL) grated **Parmesan cheese**

In saucepan, heat oil over medium-high heat; sauté onion, garlic, carrot, celery and mushrooms until no liquid remains, about 15 minutes.

Add broth, salt, pepper, nutmeg and bay leaf; cook, stirring occasionally, until reduced by half, about 5 minutes.

Add tomatoes and tomato paste; bring to boil. Reduce heat and simmer until thick enough to mound on spoon, about 20 minutes. Discard bay leaf.

Meanwhile, in large pot of boiling salted water, cook pasta until al dente, 8 to 10 minutes. Drain well; return to pot. Add sauce; toss to coat. Serve sprinkled with Parmesan cheese.

PER SERVING: about 567 cal, 23 g pro, 13 g total fat (4 g sat. fat), 93 g carb, 11 g fibre, 10 mg chol, 1,206 mg sodium. % RDI: 27% calcium, 51% iron, 65% vit A, 53% vit C, 75% folate.

Eggplant Gnocchi with Brown Butter & Pine Nut Sauce

Prep: 40 minutes   **Cook:** 55 minutes   **Makes:** 4 servings

¼ cup (60 mL) **salted butter**

¼ cup (60 mL) **pine nuts**

¼ cup (60 mL) minced **fresh parsley**

2 tbsp (30 mL) **lemon juice**

EGGPLANT GNOCCHI:

2 **eggplants** (about 2 lb/1 kg total)

1 tsp (5 mL) **salt**

2 **eggs**

2 cups (500 mL) **all-purpose flour** (approx)

EGGPLANT GNOCCHI: Peel eggplants and cut into 2-inch (5 cm) cubes. Place on 2 parchment paper–lined baking sheets; toss with salt. Roast in 350°F (180°C) oven, stirring occasionally, until very soft, about 40 minutes.

Transfer eggplant to food processor; purée until fairly smooth with some chunks. Add eggs; pulse, scraping down side of bowl occasionally, until smooth. Transfer to bowl; stir in 1½ cups (375 mL) of the flour, adding just enough of the remaining flour to create soft dough.

Turn dough out onto floured work surface; knead a few times, adding more flour if necessary to prevent sticking, just until dough holds together. Shape into 2 logs; divide each into quarters. Shape each quarter into ¾-inch (2 cm) diameter rope. With sharp knife, cut each rope on the diagonal into 1-inch (2.5 cm) pieces. (If making ahead of time, freeze on baking sheet for 2 hours or until firm; scrape into resealable freezer bags and freeze for up to 2 weeks.)

In large skillet, melt butter over medium heat; fry pine nuts until light golden and butter just begins to brown, 3 minutes. Remove from heat.

Meanwhile, in large pot of boiling salted water, cook Eggplant Gnocchi, in batches and stirring gently, until they float; boil for 5 minutes.

Return skillet to medium heat; using slotted spoon, scoop gnocchi into hot pan. Add parsley, lemon juice and ¼ cup (60 mL) of the gnocchi cooking water; toss to coat. If sauce is too thick, add up to ¼ cup (60 mL) more cooking water.

PER SERVING: about 488 cal, 12 g pro, 21 g total fat (9 g sat. fat), 65 g carb, 7 g fibre, 123 mg chol, 968 mg sodium, 400 mg potassium. % RDI: 4% calcium, 31% iron, 17% vit A, 13% vit C, 79% folate.

Spinach Pesto Fusilli with Ricotta

Prep: 12 minutes   **Cook:** 10 minutes   **Makes:** 8 servings

2 pkg (each 454 g) **fusilli**

1 bag (10 oz/284 g) **fresh spinach,** trimmed

2 tbsp (30 mL) **extra-virgin olive oil**

3 cloves **garlic,** minced

2 tbsp (30 mL) chopped **fresh basil**

1 tsp (5 mL) **salt**

½ tsp (2 mL) **pepper**

1 cup (250 mL) **ricotta cheese**

¾ cup (175 mL) grated **Parmesan cheese**

2 tbsp (30 mL) **lemon juice**

2 tbsp (30 mL) toasted **pine nuts**

In large pot of boiling salted water, cook pasta until al dente, 8 to 10 minutes. Reserving ½ cup (125 mL) of the cooking water, drain; return pasta to pot.

Meanwhile, rinse spinach; shake off excess water. In large saucepan or Dutch oven, heat half of the oil over medium heat; fry garlic, stirring, until fragrant, about 30 seconds. Stir in spinach and basil; cook, covered, for 2 minutes.

Uncover and cook, stirring, until no liquid remains, about 2 minutes. Transfer to food processor. Add remaining oil, salt and pepper; purée until smooth. Add reserved cooking water; blend well.

Add spinach mixture to fusilli along with ¾ cup (175 mL) of the ricotta cheese, Parmesan cheese and lemon juice; toss to coat. Serve topped with remaining ricotta and pine nuts.

PER SERVING: about 547 cal, 21 g pro, 12 g total fat (4 g sat. fat), 88 g carb, 6 g fibre, 19 mg chol, 722 mg sodium, 315 mg potassium. % RDI: 17% calcium, 41% iron, 40% vit A, 8% vit C, 129% folate.

Fettuccine with Green Olives, Capers & Parsley

Prep: 5 minutes   **Cook:** 12 minutes   **Makes:** 4 servings

10 oz (300 g) **fettuccine**

2 tbsp (30 mL) **extra-virgin olive oil**

2 cloves **garlic,** thinly sliced

¼ tsp (1 mL) **hot pepper flakes**

1 cup (250 mL) sliced **green olives**

⅓ cup (75 mL) chopped **fresh parsley**

2 tbsp (30 mL) **capers,** drained, rinsed and coarsely chopped

1 tsp (5 mL) grated **orange rind**

1 tbsp (15 mL) **orange juice**

In large pot of boiling salted water, cook pasta until al dente, about 8 minutes. Reserving ½ cup (125 mL) of the cooking water, drain; return pasta to pot.

Meanwhile, in large skillet, heat oil over medium heat; fry garlic and hot pepper flakes until fragrant, about 1 minute.

Add olives, half of the parsley, the capers, and orange rind and juice; cook, stirring, until heated through, about 2 minutes.

Add to pasta; toss to coat, adding enough of the reserved cooking water to moisten if necessary. Stir in remaining parsley.

PASTA

PER SERVING: about 378 cal, 10 g pro, 13 g total fat (2 g sat. fat), 56 g carb, 5 g fibre, 0 mg chol, 834 mg sodium. % RDI: 4% calcium, 23% iron, 6% vit A, 13% vit C, 70% folate.

Roasted Squash, Spinach & Three-Cheese Cannelloni

Prep: 1 hour   **Stand:** 15 minutes   **Cook:** 1½ hours   **Makes:** 10 servings

PASTA

✳ Hazelnuts add crunch to this soft, rich filling. Fresh oven-ready lasagna sheets vary in size and number per package, so you may need two packages, reserving leftover sheets and trimmings for another use.

10 sheets (8- x 6-inch/20 x 15 cm) **fresh lasagna noodles**

½ cup (125 mL) shredded **Gruyère cheese**

SQUASH FILLING:

1 **butternut squash** (about 1¼ lb/625 g)

4 cloves **garlic**

Half **onion,** cut into chunks

2 tbsp (30 mL) **olive oil**

1 tsp (5 mL) **lemon juice**

¼ tsp (1 mL) each **salt** and **pepper**

½ cup (125 mL) **ricotta cheese**

⅓ cup (75 mL) grated **Parmesan cheese**

1 tbsp (15 mL) chopped **fresh sage**

¾ cup (175 mL) coarsely chopped toasted **hazelnuts**

SPINACH FILLING:

1 pkg (1 lb/500 g) **fresh spinach,** trimmed

4 **green onions,** finely chopped

1 tbsp (15 mL) **olive oil**

½ tsp (2 mL) each **salt** and **pepper**

BÉCHAMEL SAUCE:

2 tbsp (30 mL) **butter**

3 tbsp (45 mL) **all-purpose flour**

2¼ cups (550 mL) **milk**

¼ tsp (1 mL) each **salt** and **pepper**

¼ tsp (1 mL) **nutmeg**

2 cups (500 mL) shredded **Gruyère cheese**

SQUASH FILLING: Peel and cube squash to make about 4 cups (1 L). In roasting pan, toss together squash, garlic, onion, oil, lemon juice, salt and pepper; roast in 425°F (220°C) oven until tender, about 40 minutes. Let cool.

In food processor, purée together squash mixture, ricotta and Parmesan cheeses and sage; scrape into bowl. Stir in hazelnuts.

SPINACH FILLING: Rinse spinach; shake off excess water. In Dutch oven, cook spinach, covered, over medium-high heat, stirring once, until wilted, about 5 minutes. Drain in colander; let cool. Squeeze out liquid; chop spinach. Mix together spinach, green onions, oil, salt and pepper.

BÉCHAMEL SAUCE: In saucepan, melt butter over medium heat; whisk in flour. Cook, whisking, for 2 minutes. Whisking constantly, slowly add milk; bring to boil. Reduce heat and simmer, whisking often, until bubbly and thickened, about 5 minutes. Whisk in salt, pepper and nutmeg. Remove from heat; whisk in Gruyère cheese until smooth. Spread 1 cup (250 mL) in 13- x 9-inch (3 L) glass baking dish.

Soak lasagna noodles in water until pliable, 2 minutes. Blot dry on tea towel. Cut each sheet into two 6½- x 4-inch (16 x 10 cm) rectangles.

Spread scant 3 tbsp (45 mL) of the Squash Filling along 1 short side of each rectangle, leaving ½ inch (1 cm) uncovered at ends. Top with scant 2 tbsp (30 mL) of the Spinach Filling; roll up. Arrange in baking dish. Pour remaining Béchamel Sauce over top; sprinkle with Gruyère cheese. Cover with foil.

Bake on rimmed baking sheet in 375°F (190°C) oven for 30 minutes. Uncover and bake until bubbly and cheese is lightly browned, about 20 minutes. Let stand for 5 minutes before serving.

PASTA

PER SERVING: about 503 cal, 22 g pro, 25 g total fat (10 g sat. fat), 49 g carb, 4 g fibre, 94 mg chol, 446 mg sodium. % RDI: 43% calcium, 26% iron, 96% vit A, 18% vit C, 74% folate.

TOFU, TEMPEH & SOY

Mexican Tostada Salad
(page 118)

Double-Mushroom Hot & Sour Soup

Prep: 10 minutes   **Stand:** 10 minutes   **Cook:** 10 minutes   **Makes:** 6 servings

Half pkg (½ oz/14 g pkg) **dried wood ear mushrooms**

¾ cup (175 mL) **boiling water**

3 cups (750 mL) **vegetable broth**

1 pkg (1 lb/454 g) **medium-firm tofu**, drained

1 can (8 oz/227 mL) **sliced bamboo shoots**, drained and rinsed

1 can (8 oz/227 mL) **sliced water chestnuts**, drained and rinsed

8 oz (250 g) **white** or cremini **mushrooms**, sliced

1 clove **garlic**, minced

⅓ cup (75 mL) **unseasoned rice vinegar**

3 tbsp (45 mL) **cornstarch**

3 tbsp (45 mL) **sodium-reduced soy sauce**

½ tsp (2 mL) **white** or black **pepper**

¼ tsp (1 mL) **salt**

1 cup (250 mL) **bean sprouts**

2 **green onions**, thinly sliced

2 **Thai bird's-eye peppers**, seeded and thinly sliced

1 **egg**

1 tsp (5 mL) **sesame oil**

Soak wood ear mushrooms in boiling water until softened, about 10 minutes.

In large saucepan, bring broth and 2 cups (500 mL) water to boil. Meanwhile, cut tofu and wood ear mushrooms into thin strips; add to pan along with bamboo shoots, water chestnuts and white mushrooms; return to boil.

Whisk together garlic, vinegar, cornstarch, soy sauce, pepper and salt; whisk into pan. Reduce heat and simmer, stirring, until thickened and glossy, about 3 minutes. Stir in bean sprouts, green onions and Thai peppers; simmer for 1 minute.

Whisk egg; stirring constantly, slowly pour into soup. Cook until egg sets in strands and floats to surface, about 2 minutes. Drizzle with sesame oil.

* Wood ear mushrooms are also known as black fungus or tree ear mushrooms. Find them, along with other ingredients needed for this soup, in some supermarkets or Asian food stores. If desired, the soup can be thinned with a bit of additional vegetable broth.

TOFU, TEMPEH & SOY

PER SERVING: about 139 cal, 10 g pro, 5 g total fat (1 g sat. fat), 16 g carb, 3 g fibre, 31 mg chol, 703 mg sodium, 451 mg potassium. % RDI: 17% calcium, 16% iron, 6% vit A, 15% vit C, 18% folate.

Edamame Vegetable Soup with Wasabi Cream

Prep: 12 minutes **Cook:** 20 minutes **Makes:** 6 to 8 servings

* This soup is also lovely without the wasabi cream topping, as in our photo (opposite).

1 tbsp (15 mL) **olive oil**
2 **carrots,** thinly sliced
2 stalks **celery,** thinly sliced
1 **onion,** diced
2 cloves **garlic,** minced
¼ tsp (1 mL) **pepper**
3 cups (750 mL) **vegetable broth**
1 **zucchini,** thinly sliced
Half **sweet red pepper,** diced
2 tbsp (30 mL) **sodium-reduced soy sauce**
1½ tsp (7 mL) grated **fresh ginger**

½ tsp (2 mL) **sesame oil**
Half pkg (1 lb/454 g pkg) **medium-firm tofu,** drained
1 cup (250 mL) frozen **shelled soybeans** (edamame), thawed

WASABI CREAM:
½ cup (125 mL) **sour cream**
2 tsp (10 mL) minced **fresh chives,** green onions or fresh parsley
1 tsp (5 mL) **lemon juice**
1 tsp (5 mL) **wasabi paste**

WASABI CREAM: Mix together sour cream, chives, lemon juice and wasabi. Set aside in refrigerator.

In Dutch oven or large saucepan, heat olive oil over medium heat; fry carrots, celery, onion, garlic and pepper, stirring occasionally, until softened, about 8 minutes.

Add broth, 3 cups (750 mL) water, zucchini, red pepper, soy sauce, ginger and sesame oil; bring to boil. Reduce heat and simmer until carrots are tender, about 8 minutes.

Cut tofu into ½-inch (1 cm) cubes. Add to soup along with soybeans; simmer for 3 minutes.

Ladle into bowls; top with Wasabi Cream.

PER EACH OF 8 SERVINGS: about 108 cal, 5 g pro, 6 g total fat (2 g sat. fat), 9 g carb, 2 g fibre, 6 mg chol, 393 mg sodium, 328 mg potassium. % RDI: 10% calcium, 9% iron, 41% vit A, 30% vit C, 31% folate.

Mexican Tostada Salad

Prep: 15 minutes   **Cook:** 10 minutes   **Makes:** 5 servings

✳ Layered with taco-style ingredients, this colourful salad is bursting with fresh market vegetables. Sturdier lettuce, such as iceberg, romaine or leaf, is best here. No tostadas? Use handfuls of tortilla chips or broken taco shells.If desired, garnish with spoonfuls of sour cream or plain yogurt and lime wedges.

2 tbsp (30 mL) **vegetable oil**
Half **onion,** diced
2 cloves **garlic,** minced
2 tsp (10 mL) **chili powder**
½ tsp (2 mL) **ground coriander**
1 pkg (340 g) **precooked soy protein mixture** (such as Yves Veggie Ground Round)
¾ cup (175 mL) **tomato juice**
5 cups (1.25 L) shredded **lettuce**
10 **tostadas**

½ cup (125 mL) **salsa**
½ cup (125 mL) shredded **old Cheddar cheese** or Monterey Jack cheese
1 **avocado,** peeled, pitted and chopped
2 **plum** or vine-ripened **tomatoes,** chopped
2 **green onions,** sliced

In skillet, heat oil over medium heat; fry onion and garlic, stirring occasionally, for 3 minutes. Add chili powder and coriander; fry until onion is softened, about 2 minutes. Add soy protein mixture and tomato juice, breaking up soy mixture with spoon. Cook until very thick, about 5 minutes.

Place small handful lettuce on each of 5 plates or shallow bowls. Top each with 1 of the tostadas, another handful of the remaining lettuce, ¼ cup (60 mL) of the soy protein mixture, then some each of the salsa, cheese, avocado, tomatoes and green onions. Repeat layers once.

PER SERVING: about 376 cal, 19 g pro, 22 g total fat (5 g sat. fat), 29 g carb, 10 g fibre, 12 mg chol, 788 mg sodium, 865 mg potassium. % RDI: 17% calcium, 34% iron, 14% vit A, 25% vit C, 37% folate.

Tofu Salad Sandwiches

Prep: 8 minutes   **Makes:** 4 servings

1 pkg (425 g) **firm tofu**, drained

½ cup (125 mL) **light mayonnaise**

¼ cup (60 mL) finely diced **dill pickles**

1 **green onion,** minced

1 tsp (5 mL) chopped **fresh dill** or parsley

1 tsp (5 mL) **Dijon mustard**

½ tsp (2 mL) **turmeric**

½ tsp (2 mL) each **salt** and **pepper**

8 slices **multigrain bread**

1 **tomato,** sliced

4 leaves **lettuce**

* This creamy filling looks just like egg salad and bursts with fresh dill and dill pickle flavours. If you like, add alfalfa sprouts when assembling the sandwiches.

Pat tofu dry. With fork, mash tofu until crumbly; stir in mayonnaise, pickles, green onion, dill, mustard, turmeric, salt and pepper. (To store, refrigerate filling, covered, for up to 3 days.)

Spread over 4 of the bread slices; top with tomato, lettuce and remaining bread.

TOFU, TEMPEH & SOY

PER SERVING: about 423 cal, 18 g pro, 19 g total fat (3 g sat. fat), 50 g carb, 8 g fibre, 11 mg chol, 1,079 mg sodium. % RDI: 25% calcium, 39% iron, 5% vit A, 15% vit C, 70% folate.

Five-Spice Tofu Stir-Fry

Prep: 12 minutes   **Cook:** 12 minutes   **Makes:** 4 servings

½ cup (125 mL) **vegetable broth**

2 tbsp (30 mL) **vegetarian oyster sauce**

1 tbsp (15 mL) **cornstarch**

1 tbsp (15 mL) **sodium-reduced soy sauce**

1 tsp (5 mL) packed **brown sugar**

1 pkg (1 lb/454 g) **medium-firm tofu,** drained

½ tsp (2 mL) **five-spice powder**

2 tbsp (30 mL) **vegetable oil**

3 cloves **garlic,** thinly sliced

¼ tsp (1 mL) **hot pepper flakes**

1 head **bok choy** (1 lb/500 g), chopped

8 oz (250 g) **shiitake mushrooms,** stemmed and halved

Whisk together broth, oyster sauce, cornstarch, soy sauce, sugar and ½ cup (125 mL) water.

Cut tofu into 1-inch (2.5 cm) cubes; gently toss with five-spice powder. In wok or skillet, heat half of the oil over medium-high heat; stir-fry tofu until golden, about 4 minutes. Transfer to paper towel–lined plate.

Heat remaining oil over medium-high heat; stir-fry garlic and hot pepper flakes for 30 seconds. Add bok choy and mushrooms; stir-fry for 3 minutes.

Stir in tofu and broth mixture; bring to boil. Reduce heat and simmer, covered, until sauce is thickened and vegetables are softened, about 3 minutes.

TOFU, TEMPEH & SOY

PER SERVING: about 192 cal, 12 g pro, 11 g total fat (1 g sat. fat), 14 g carb, 4 g fibre, 1 mg chol, 542 mg sodium, 780 mg potassium. % RDI: 23% calcium, 22% iron, 53% vit A, 55% vit C, 50% folate.

Thai Green Curry with Tofu & Vegetables

Prep: 15 minutes **Stand:** 30 minutes **Cook:** 15 minutes **Makes:** 4 servings

1 pkg (1 lb/454 g) **medium-firm tofu**

1 large **Japanese eggplant** (8 oz/250 mL)

1 tbsp (15 mL) **vegetable oil**

⅓ cup (75 mL) **Thai Green Curry Paste** (page 272)

¾ tsp (4 mL) **salt**

2 cans (each 400 mL) **coconut milk**

½ cup (125 mL) **vegetable broth**

1 cup (250 mL) halved (crosswise) **green beans**

1 cup (250 mL) frozen **whole okra,** thawed and halved lengthwise

¼ cup (60 mL) chopped **fresh coriander**

1 tbsp (15 mL) **lime juice**

Drain tofu between 2 paper towel–lined plates for 30 minutes. Cut tofu and eggplant into ¾-inch (2 cm) cubes.

In large shallow Dutch oven, heat oil over medium heat; fry curry paste and ¼ tsp (1 mL) of the salt, stirring, for 2 minutes. Stir in coconut milk and broth; bring to boil.

Add tofu, eggplant, green beans and remaining salt. Reduce heat and simmer, covered and stirring occasionally, until eggplant is tender, about 8 minutes.

Add okra and coriander; simmer for 1 minute. Stir in lime juice.

PER SERVING: about 571 cal, 13 g pro, 53 g total fat (41 g sat. fat), 21 g carb, 6 g fibre, 0 mg chol, 594 mg sodium. % RDI: 19% calcium, 67% iron, 7% vit A, 22% vit C, 60% folate.

Stir-Fried Soy & Tofu

Prep: 10 minutes   **Cook:** 20 minutes   **Makes:** 4 servings

3 tbsp (45 mL) **sodium-reduced soy sauce**

2 tbsp (30 mL) **cornstarch**

2 tbsp (30 mL) **black bean garlic sauce**

2 tbsp (30 mL) **vegetarian oyster sauce** or hoisin sauce

½ tsp (2 mL) **Asian chili paste** or hot pepper sauce

1 tbsp (15 mL) **vegetable oil**

1 **carrot,** diced

1½ cups (375 mL) sliced **white mushrooms**

6 **green onions** (white and light green parts separated), sliced

3 cloves **garlic,** minced

1 tbsp (15 mL) minced **fresh ginger**

⅛ tsp (0.5 mL) **ground cloves**

⅛ tsp (0.5 mL) **pepper**

1 pkg (340 g) **precooked soy protein mixture** (such as Yves Veggie Ground Round)

1 pkg (1 lb/454 g) **medium-firm tofu,** drained and cut into ¾-inch (2 cm) cubes

¾ cup (175 mL) frozen **shelled soybeans** (edamame) or peas, thawed

Whisk together soy sauce, cornstarch, black bean garlic sauce, oyster sauce and chili paste.

In wok or large skillet, heat oil over medium-high heat; stir-fry carrot, mushrooms, white parts of onions, garlic, ginger, cloves and pepper until vegetables are softened, about 6 minutes.

Stir in soy protein mixture; cook until heated through, about 2 minutes. Stir in soy sauce mixture and 1¾ cups (425 mL) water; bring to boil. Add tofu; reduce heat and simmer, covered, until thickened, about 10 minutes.

Stir in soybeans and green parts of onions; cook until heated through, about 2 minutes.

PER SERVING: about 300 cal, 30 g pro, 10 g total fat (1 g sat. fat), 25 g carb, 9 g fibre, 0 mg chol, 1,236 mg sodium, 891 mg potassium. % RDI: 31% calcium, 59% iron, 34% vit A, 12% vit C, 52% folate.

Spaghetti & Tofu Balls

Prep: 20 minutes   **Stand:** 1 hour   **Cook:** 25 minutes   **Makes:** 6 servings

1 pkg (350 g) **firm** or extra-firm **tofu,** drained

⅓ cup (75 mL) chopped **fresh parsley**

1½ cups (375 mL) **dry bread crumbs**

2 tbsp (30 mL) **tahini** or almond butter

2 tbsp (30 mL) **soy sauce**

1 tbsp (15 mL) **Dijon mustard**

¼ tsp (1 mL) **pepper**

2 cloves **garlic,** minced

2 tbsp (30 mL) **olive oil**

Marinara Sauce (page 271) or 4 cups (1 L) tomato pasta sauce

12 oz (375 g) **spaghetti**

⅓ cup (75 mL) grated **Parmesan cheese** (optional)

In food processor, purée tofu with parsley until crumbly. Add bread crumbs, tahini, soy sauce, mustard, pepper and garlic; pulse to combine. Roll by 1 tbsp (15 mL) into balls. Refrigerate for 1 hour or, covered, up to 24 hours.

In large nonstick skillet, heat half of the oil over medium heat. In batches and adding remaining oil as needed, cook tofu balls, stirring often, until golden, about 8 minutes.

In large saucepan, heat Marinara Sauce over medium heat until steaming. Add tofu balls; reduce heat and simmer until heated through, about 5 minutes.

Meanwhile, in large pot of boiling salted water, cook pasta until al dente, about 8 minutes. Drain; transfer to platter. Spoon sauce over top; sprinkle with Parmesan cheese (if using).

PER SERVING: about 516 cal, 18 g pro, 16 g total fat (2 g sat. fat), 77 g carb, 7 g fibre, 0 mg chol, 1,284 mg sodium. % RDI: 22% calcium, 46% iron, 44% vit A, 72% vit C, 75% folate.

TOFU, TEMPEH & SOY

Braised Tofu Napa Nabe

Prep: 10 minutes   **Cook:** 25 minutes   **Makes:** 6 servings

1 small head **napa cabbage**
   (about 1½ lb/750 g)
1 **Spanish** or sweet **onion**
8 oz (250 g) **shiitake mushrooms**
3 cups (750 mL) **vegetable broth**

1 pkg (1 lb/454 g) **soft** or medium-
   firm **tofu,** drained and cubed
¼ cup (60 mL) **mirin**
¼ cup (60 mL) **soy sauce**
1 **green onion,** sliced
Ponzu sauce

Chop cabbage to make about 8 cups (2 L). Halve onion; cut into ½-inch (1 cm) thick slices. Remove and discard mushroom stems; thickly slice caps.

Place cabbage and onion in Dutch oven; sprinkle with mushrooms. Pour in broth and 3 cups (750 mL) water; bring to boil, covered. Reduce heat and simmer, covered, until vegetables are softened, about 15 minutes.

Add tofu, mirin and soy sauce; simmer until tofu is heated through, about 5 minutes. Sprinkle with green onion. Serve with ponzu sauce for dipping tofu and vegetables.

* *Nabe* is a Japanese pot used for braising, and for making stews and casseroles. *Mirin* is Japanese sweet rice wine and *ponzu* is a Japanese sauce made with *yuzu,* a type of citrus fruit. All are available in Asian and specialty food markets and some grocery stores. Serve this dish with steamed Japanese rice.

TOFU, TEMPEH & SOY

PER SERVING: about 110 cal, 9 g pro, 3 g total fat (trace sat. fat), 14 g carb, 4 g fibre, 2 mg chol, 1,000 mg sodium, 370 mg potassium. % RDI: 11% calcium, 14% iron, 4% vit A, 10% vit C, 37% folate.

Miso-Glazed Tofu Vegetable Brochettes with Soba Noodles

Prep: 25 minutes   **Stand:** 15 minutes   **Cook:** 20 minutes   **Makes:** 4 servings

✳ To make these indoors, sear brochettes in large greased skillet over medium heat, turning often, until tender, about 18 minutes. Serve with Soba Noodles (opposite).

1 **sweet potato** (8 oz/250 g)

1 pkg (350 g) **extra-firm tofu,** drained

1 **Japanese eggplant**

¼ cup (60 mL) **white miso paste**

3 tbsp (45 mL) **vegetable oil**

1 tbsp (15 mL) **granulated sugar**

2 tsp (10 mL) minced **fresh ginger**

1 tsp (5 mL) **sesame oil**

16 **cremini** or white **mushrooms,** stemmed

Peel sweet potato and cut into 1½-inch (4 cm) cubes; microwave at high for 1 minute.

Pat tofu dry; cut into 1½-inch (4 cm) cubes. Cut eggplant into ½-inch (1 cm) thick rounds; add to sweet potatoes along with tofu.

Stir together miso, vegetable oil, 2 tbsp (30 mL) water, sugar, ginger and sesame oil; add to eggplant mixture along with mushrooms. Toss to coat; let stand for 15 minutes.

Thread tofu and vegetables onto skewers; brush with any remaining marinade. Grill, covered, on greased grill over medium heat, turning often, until vegetables are tender, about 18 minutes.

PER SERVING: about 311 cal, 14 g pro, 18 g total fat (2 g sat. fat), 28 g carb, 5 g fibre, 0 mg chol, 659 mg sodium. % RDI: 15% calcium, 20% iron, 118% vit A, 17% vit C, 19% folate.

SOBA NOODLES

Prep: 5 minutes   **Cook:** 8 minutes   **Makes:** 4 servings

In saucepan of boiling water, cook 1 pkg (250 g) Japanese soba (buckwheat) noodles, stirring gently, until tender, about 8 minutes. Drain and chill under cold water; drain well.

Serve with 1 cup (250 mL) prepared soba noodle dipping sauce; 1 green onion, thinly sliced; and dab wasabi paste.

* Look for soba noodles and dipping sauce in the sushi or Asian section of natural food and grocery stores.

TOFU, TEMPEH & SOY

Miso-Glazed Tofu Vegetable
Brochettes with Soba Noodles
(page 128)

Vegetarian Tourtière

Prep: 30 minutes **Stand:** 40 minutes **Cook:** 2 hours **Makes:** 8 servings

✳ Being vegetarian doesn't mean you have to skip the tourtière. For a vegan version, replace butter in crust with additional shortening. Serve this densely textured flaky pie with Tomato Pear Chutney (page 278).

2 cups (500 mL) **TVP granules**

1 cup (250 mL) **boiling water**

2 tbsp (30 mL) **vegetable oil**

3 stalks **celery** (with leaves), diced

2 **onions,** diced

2 cloves **garlic,** minced

2 cups (500 mL) cubed peeled **potatoes**

2 tsp (10 mL) **tamari** or sodium-reduced soy sauce

1½ tsp (7 mL) **dried savory**

½ tsp (2 mL) each **salt** and **pepper**

¼ tsp (1 mL) **ground allspice**

¼ tsp (1 mL) **ground cloves**

2 **bay leaves**

2 cups (500 mL) **vegetable broth**

PEPPER THYME PASTRY:

3 cups (750 mL) **all-purpose flour**

1 tsp (5 mL) **salt**

1 tsp (5 mL) **dried thyme**

½ tsp (2 mL) **cracked black peppercorns**

½ cup (125 mL) cold **unsalted butter,** cubed

½ cup (125 mL) cold **shortening,** cubed

2 tsp (10 mL) **vinegar**

Ice water

PEPPER THYME PASTRY: Whisk together flour, salt, thyme and pepper. With pastry blender or 2 knives, cut in butter and shortening until in fine crumbs with a few larger pieces. In liquid measure, whisk vinegar with enough ice water to make ⅔ cup (150 mL). Drizzle over flour mixture, tossing with fork to form ragged dough.

Divide in half; press into 2 discs. Wrap separately; refrigerate until chilled, about 30 minutes, or up to 24 hours.

Place TVP in large bowl; pour boiling water over top. Let stand, covered, for 10 minutes.

Meanwhile, in shallow Dutch oven, heat oil over medium-high heat; sauté celery, onions and garlic until golden, about 10 minutes. Stir in potatoes, tamari, savory, salt, pepper, allspice, cloves, bay leaves and TVP; cook, stirring often, for 5 minutes.

Stir in broth and 1 cup (250 mL) water; bring to boil. Reduce heat and simmer, covered, until potatoes are tender, 30 to 40 minutes.

Break up most of the potatoes with back of spoon; simmer, uncovered, until slightly thickened, 7 to 10 minutes. Let cool.

On lightly floured surface, roll out each pastry disc to 10-inch (25 cm) circle. Fit 1 into 9-inch (23 cm) pie plate; trim overhang even with rim. Spoon in filling. Lightly brush rim with water; top with remaining pastry. Trim edge; flute or use fork to seal. Brush with water; cut steam vents in top.

Bake in bottom third of 400°F (200°C) oven until golden, about 1 hour. Let stand for 10 minutes before slicing.

PER SERVING: about 478 cal, 17 g pro, 24 g total fat (9 g sat. fat), 49 g carb, 7 g fibre, 27 mg chol, 636 mg sodium. % RDI: 10% calcium, 36% iron, 10% vit A, 7% vit C, 41% folate.

Baked Tofu with Steamed Sesame Bok Choy

Prep: 10 minutes **Stand:** 1 hour **Cook:** 30 minutes **Makes:** 4 servings

1 pkg (1 lb/454 g) **firm tofu,** drained

¼ cup (60 mL) **sodium-reduced soy sauce**

2 tbsp (30 mL) **hoisin sauce**

1 clove **garlic,** minced

½ tsp (2 mL) **sesame oil**

¼ tsp (1 mL) **Asian chili paste** or hot pepper sauce

2 tsp (10 mL) **vegetable oil**

2 cups (500 mL) sliced **shiitake mushroom caps** or cremini mushrooms

1 tbsp (15 mL) minced **fresh ginger**

4 **baby bok choy**

1 **sweet red pepper,** thinly sliced

½ cup (125 mL) **vegetable broth**

2 **green onions,** sliced

2 tsp (10 mL) toasted **sesame seeds**

Cut tofu in half horizontally. In 8-inch (2 L) square glass baking dish, whisk together soy and hoisin sauces, garlic, sesame oil and chili paste. Add tofu; turn to coat. Let stand for 1 hour or, refrigerated, up to 24 hours.

Bake in 350°F (180°C) oven, turning once, until golden, about 30 minutes. Reserving cooking liquid, cut tofu crosswise into ¾-inch (2 cm) slices. Cover; keep warm.

Meanwhile, in large skillet, heat oil over medium-high heat; sauté mushrooms and ginger until mushrooms are golden, about 5 minutes. Cut bok choy lengthwise into quarters. Add to skillet along with red pepper and broth; bring to boil. Steam, covered, for 2 minutes. Uncover and add green onions; cook until bok choy is tender, about 2 minutes.

Reserving cooking liquid, remove vegetables from pan; arrange on platter. Top with tofu. Whisk reserved tofu cooking liquid into vegetable cooking liquid. Drizzle over tofu; sprinkle with sesame seeds.

PER SERVING: about 185 cal, 13 g pro, 10 g total fat (2 g sat. fat), 14 g carb, 3 g fibre, 0 mg chol, 913 mg sodium. % RDI: 22% calcium, 26% iron, 32% vit A, 118% vit C, 33% folate.

Spicy Stir-Fried Cabbage, Tofu & Peanuts

Prep: 15 minutes   **Cook:** 10 minutes   **Makes:** 4 servings

2 tbsp (30 mL) **black bean garlic sauce**

2 tsp (10 mL) **Chinese black vinegar** or balsamic vinegar

1 tsp (5 mL) **granulated sugar**

2 tbsp (30 mL) **peanut** or vegetable **oil**

3 **green onions,** thinly sliced

3 cloves **garlic,** minced

1 **red** or green **hot pepper,** minced

2 tsp (10 mL) minced **fresh ginger**

1 pkg (350 g) **extra-firm tofu,** drained and cubed

8 cups (2 L) coarsely chopped **green cabbage** (half head)

½ cup (125 mL) unsalted **roasted peanuts**

½ tsp (2 mL) **ground Szechuan pepper** (optional)

1 tsp (5 mL) **sesame oil**

Mix together black bean garlic sauce, vinegar, sugar and 3 tbsp (45 mL) water.

In wok or large saucepan, heat peanut oil over high heat; stir-fry onions, garlic, hot pepper and ginger until fragrant, about 1 minute.

Stir in tofu. Add cabbage; stir-fry until beginning to wilt, about 3 minutes.

Add black bean sauce mixture; stir-fry until cabbage is tender and no liquid remains, 3 to 5 minutes.

Stir in peanuts, and Szechuan pepper (if using); cook just until heated through. Stir in sesame oil.

PER SERVING: about 323 cal, 16 g pro, 23 g total fat (3 g sat. fat), 18 g carb, 5 g fibre, 0 mg chol, 148 mg sodium. % RDI: 18% calcium, 16% iron, 5% vit A, 58% vit C, 35% folate.

Tahini Carrot Tofu Patties

Prep: 25 minutes   **Cook:** 18 minutes   **Makes:** 4 servings

✳ Serve patties over warmed Marinara Sauce (page 271) or tomato pasta sauce, or with salad greens.

3 tbsp (45 mL) **olive oil**

1 **onion,** chopped

½ cup (125 mL) grated **carrot**

2 cloves **garlic,** minced

¼ tsp (1 mL) **ground cumin**

Pinch **cayenne pepper**

1 pkg (350 g) **extra-firm tofu,** drained

3 tbsp (45 mL) **tahini**

¼ cup (60 mL) chopped **fresh parsley**

¼ cup (60 mL) **dry bread crumbs**

2 tbsp (30 mL) **lemon juice**

¼ tsp (1 mL) each **salt** and **pepper**

In skillet, heat 1 tbsp (15 mL) of the oil over medium heat; fry onion, carrot, garlic, cumin and cayenne, stirring occasionally, until onion is softened, about 5 minutes.

In food processor, purée tofu with tahini. Add onion mixture, parsley, bread crumbs, lemon juice, salt and pepper; pulse to combine. Form into eight ½-inch (1 cm) thick patties.

Heat half of the remaining oil in large nonstick skillet over medium heat; fry half of the patties, turning once, until golden, about 6 minutes. Repeat with remaining oil and patties.

PER SERVING: about 289 cal, 13 g pro, 22 g total fat (3 g sat. fat), 14 g carb, 3 g fibre, 0 mg chol, 226 mg sodium, 286 mg potassium. % RDI: 19% calcium, 24% iron, 25% vit A, 15% vit C, 24% folate.

Veggie "Chicken" Chili

Prep: 8 minutes   **Cook:** 25 minutes   **Makes:** 6 to 8 servings

2 tbsp (30 mL) **vegetable oil**

1 **onion,** chopped

3 cloves **garlic,** minced

2 tsp (10 mL) **dried oregano**

¼ tsp (1 mL) **salt**

3 tbsp (45 mL) **tomato paste**

3 tbsp (45 mL) **chili powder**

2 tsp (10 mL) **ground cumin**

1 can (28 oz/796 mL) **diced tomatoes**

1 can (19 oz/540 mL) **white kidney beans,** drained and rinsed

½ cup (125 mL) **tomato juice**

2 pkg (each 340 g) **precooked chicken-flavour soy protein mixture** (such as Yves Veggie Ground Chicken)

TORTILLA CRISPS:

2 large (10-inch/25 cm) **flour tortillas**

1 tsp (5 mL) **vegetable oil**

> ✳ Serve steaming hot bowls of this family-friendly "not-chicken" chili with a selection of toppers, such as pickled jalapeño peppers, shredded Cheddar cheese, sliced green onions and sour cream.

In Dutch oven or large saucepan, heat oil over medium heat; fry onion, garlic, oregano and salt, stirring occasionally, until onion is softened, about 5 minutes. Stir in tomato paste, chili powder and cumin; cook for 1 minute.

Add tomatoes, beans, tomato juice and soy protein mixture, breaking up with spoon; bring to boil. Reduce heat and simmer, stirring occasionally, until thickened, about 15 minutes.

TORTILLA CRISPS: Meanwhile, brush tortillas with oil; stack and cut into 12 pieces to make 24 wedges total. Arrange in single layer on baking sheet. Bake in 350°F (180°C) oven until crisp, 8 to 10 minutes. Serve with chili.

PER EACH OF 8 SERVINGS: about 295 cal, 22 g pro, 8 g total fat (1 g sat. fat), 34 g carb, 12 g fibre, 0 mg chol, 1,070 mg sodium, 896 mg potassium. % RDI: 14% calcium, 63% iron, 11% vit A, 32% vit C, 25% folate.

Tempeh Country Pâté

Prep: 15 minutes   **Stand:** 2½ hours   **Cook:** 1¼ hours
Makes: about 3 cups (750 mL)

2 tbsp (30 mL) **olive oil**
1 cup (250 mL) chopped **shallots**
   or onion
½ cup (125 mL) chopped **celery**
1 clove **garlic,** minced
1 tbsp (15 mL) chopped **fresh**
   thyme
1 pkg (8 oz/240 g) **tempeh**

½ cup (125 mL) **brandy**
3 tbsp (45 mL) **tamari** or soy sauce
1 cup (250 mL) finely chopped
   walnuts
1 tbsp (15 mL) **Dijon mustard**
1 tbsp (15 mL) **green peppercorns**
   in brine, drained and rinsed

In saucepan, heat oil over medium heat; fry shallots, celery, garlic and thyme, stirring often, until softened, about 8 minutes.

Crumble tempeh; stir into pan along with brandy, tamari and 3 tbsp (45 mL) water; bring to boil. Reduce heat and simmer, covered, until only 1 tbsp (15 mL) liquid remains, about 10 minutes.

Scrape into food processor. Add half of the walnuts and the mustard; purée until smooth. Stir in green peppercorns.

Grease three 1-cup (250 mL) ramekins; divide remaining walnuts among ramekins. Scrape tempeh mixture into ramekins, smoothing tops. Place on small baking sheet; cover with foil.

Bake in 350°F (180°C) oven for 30 minutes. Uncover and bake until edges are golden and centres are firm to the touch, about 15 minutes. Let cool on rack. Run knife around sides to loosen. Refrigerate, covered, for 2 hours or up to 3 days. (Or, overwrap with plastic wrap and foil and freeze for up to 1 month.)

To serve, invert onto plate.

* Here, tempeh combines with walnuts and brined green peppercorns to make a chunky-smooth pâté to spread on flatbread or sliced baguette. Serve with red currant or red pepper jelly for a touch of sweetness.

PER 1 TBSP (15 ML): about 36 cal, 1 g pro, 3 g total fat (trace sat. fat), 2 g carb, trace fibre, 0 mg chol, 68 mg sodium. % RDI: 1% calcium, 2% iron, 1% vit A, 3% folate.

Tempeh Chili sin Carne

Prep: 12 minutes   **Cook:** 1¼ hours   **Makes:** 6 to 8 servings

* No tempeh? It can be replaced with 1 package (1 lb/ 454 g) medium-firm tofu, drained and diced or crumbled.

2 tbsp (30 mL) **vegetable** or olive **oil**

1 large **onion,** diced

3 cloves **garlic,** minced

1 tbsp (15 mL) **ancho chili powder** or chili powder

1 tbsp (15 mL) **cocoa powder**

1 tsp (5 mL) **ground cumin**

1 tsp (5 mL) **dried oregano**

¾ tsp (4 mL) **salt**

¼ tsp (1 mL) **pepper**

1 cup (250 mL) **vegetable broth** or water

2 pkg (each 8 oz/240 g) **tempeh,** cut into 1-inch (2.5 cm) pieces

2 cans (each 28 oz/796 mL) **diced tomatoes**

1 can (19 oz/540 mL) **red kidney beans,** drained and rinsed

1 can (19 oz/540 mL) **black beans,** drained and rinsed

2 tbsp (30 mL) chopped **canned chipotle peppers** with adobo sauce

1 tbsp (15 mL) **liquid honey**

⅓ cup (75 mL) chopped **fresh coriander**

In Dutch oven, heat oil over medium heat; fry onion and garlic, stirring occasionally, until onion is softened, about 5 minutes.

Add chili powder, cocoa powder, cumin, oregano, salt and pepper; cook, stirring, for 1 minute. Stir in vegetable broth, scraping up any brown bits from bottom of pot.

Stir in tempeh, tomatoes, kidney and black beans, chipotle peppers and honey; bring to boil. Reduce heat and simmer, stirring occasionally, until slightly thickened, about 1 hour. Sprinkle with coriander.

PER EACH OF 8 SERVINGS: about 301 cal, 19 g pro, 11 g total fat (2 g sat. fat), 38 g carb, 10 g fibre, 0 mg chol, 945 mg sodium, 963 mg potassium. % RDI: 15% calcium, 38% iron, 9% vit A, 52% vit C, 37% folate.

TOFU, TEMPEH & TVP

TOFU

Tofu, or bean curd, is a white, custardlike block sold in varying degrees of firmness. It's made by curdling puréed soaked soybeans with a coagulant such as magnesium chloride and pressing the mixture into moulds. The whey is drained off, leaving a block of the solids.

Tofu is perishable and should be stored in clean water (change it daily). You can keep it in the refrigerator for up to 1 week. While you can freeze tofu, it will get chewier.

There are two main types of tofu: regular and silken. Regular tofus vary in firmness from soft to extra-firm. Firmer tofus are best for grilling, stir-frying, searing, roasting or deep-frying, while softer ones work well in soups. Silken tofu is known for its delicate creaminess, making it lovely to use in dressings and desserts. Or you can enjoy silken tofu as is, with just a drizzle of soy sauce and a sprinkle of sliced green onions. If a recipe doesn't specify which type of tofu to use, choose medium-firm.

TEMPEH

Tempeh is made from soybeans (or soybeans mixed with grains), which have been cultured and fermented. It is sold in cakes in many health food stores – often frozen, as it is quite perishable. Freezing does not have an adverse effect on the texture.

Tempeh has a nutty mushroom flavour and a medium-firm texture. It can be sliced, crumbled or cubed; and marinated, fried, steamed, grilled or roasted. Use tempeh in chilis, stuffings and soups, or puréed as the base for spreads.

TVP

Textured vegetable protein (TVP), is a dried soy product available in granules or chunks that, when cooked, resemble the texture of ground meat. Available in health food stores, the health food section of grocery stores, and bulk food stores, TVP is an economical way to get protein into a vegetarian diet. Like tofu, TVP has a mild flavour and absorbs the flavours it's cooked with.

Tofu Scramble & Tempeh "Bacon"

Prep: 12 minutes   **Stand:** 2 hours   **Cook:** 25 minutes   **Makes:** 4 servings

* This eggless, meatless take on diner-style scrambled eggs and bacon needs only a slice of toast and a cup of coffee or juice alongside.

2 tbsp (30 mL) **olive oil**

2 **green onions,** thinly sliced

Half **sweet red pepper,** diced

1½ tsp (7 mL) **ground cumin**

1 tsp (5 mL) **ground coriander**

1 tsp (5 mL) **turmeric**

1 pkg (1 lb/454 g) **medium-firm** or firm **tofu,** drained and crumbled

1 tbsp (15 mL) **sodium-reduced soy sauce**

½ tsp (2 mL) **hot sauce** (optional)

TEMPEH "BACON":

¼ cup (60 mL) **boiling water**

2 tbsp (30 mL) **olive oil**

3 tbsp (45 mL) **sodium-reduced soy sauce**

2 tsp (10 mL) **maple syrup** or liquid honey

2 tsp (10 mL) **apple cider vinegar**

½ tsp (2 mL) **ancho chili powder,** chipotle chili powder or chili powder

1 drop **liquid smoke** (optional)

1 pkg (8 oz/240 g) **tempeh,** cut into ¼-inch (5 mm) thick strips

TEMPEH "BACON": In shallow glass dish, combine boiling water, ½ tsp (2 mL) of the oil, soy sauce, maple syrup, vinegar, chili powder, and liquid smoke (if using); add tempeh, turning to coat. Refrigerate, covered and turning once or twice, for at least 2 hours or up to 2 days.

Reserving marinade, drain tempeh. In large nonstick skillet, heat remaining oil over medium-high heat; fry tempeh, in 2 batches, turning once, until golden, about 5 minutes. Arrange in single layer on greased baking sheet. Just before serving, reheat in 300°F (150°C) oven until hot, about 5 minutes.

In nonstick wok or large skillet, heat oil over medium-high heat; fry onions, pepper, cumin, coriander and turmeric until softened, about 3 minutes. Add tofu, reserved marinade, soy sauce, and hot sauce (if using); cook, tossing to coat, until no liquid remains, 3 to 5 minutes. Serve with Tempeh "Bacon."

PER SERVING: about 340 cal, 21 g pro, 25 g total fat (5 g sat. fat), 14 g carb, 2 g fibre, 0 mg chol, 629 mg sodium, 517 mg potassium. % RDI: 28% calcium, 33% iron, 7% vit A, 43% vit C, 20% folate.

Tempeh & Rice–Stuffed Peppers

Prep: 20 minutes   **Stand:** 20 minutes   **Cook:** 1¾ hours   **Makes:** 6 servings

✻ Partially freezing tempeh makes grating it a cinch. Nutritional yeast adds a savoury cheese-like dimension to the filling – look for it in health food stores. Use medium-size green, red, yellow or orange peppers with flat bottoms.

6 **sweet peppers**

1 cup (250 mL) **long-grain rice,** rinsed and drained

¼ tsp (1 mL) **salt**

2 pkg (each 8 oz/240 g) **tempeh**

¼ cup (60 mL) **olive oil**

1 **onion,** finely diced

1 stalk **celery,** finely diced

3 cloves **garlic,** minced

¼ cup (60 mL) **dry white wine** or tomato juice

3 tbsp (45 mL) **sodium-reduced soy sauce**

2 tsp (10 mL) **dried oregano**

1 tsp (5 mL) **salt**

½ tsp (2 mL) **pepper**

¼ cup (60 mL) chopped **fresh parsley**

¼ cup (60 mL) **nutritional yeast** (optional)

1 can (28 oz/796 mL) **crushed tomatoes**

2 **bay leaves**

1 sprig **fresh basil**

About 1 inch (2.5 cm) down from stem end, slice tops off peppers. Reserve tops; scrape out ribs and seeds from peppers.

In saucepan, bring 1½ cups (375 mL) water, rice and salt to boil. Reduce heat; simmer, covered, until no liquid remains, 20 minutes. Remove from heat; let stand, covered, for 10 minutes. Scrape into bowl; let cool.

Using coarse side of box grater, grate tempeh. In large skillet, heat half of the oil over medium heat; fry onion, celery and garlic until softened, about 5 minutes. Add tempeh, wine, soy sauce, oregano, salt and pepper. Cook until no liquid remains, about 1 minute.

Scrape over rice. Add parsley, and yeast (if using); toss to combine. Divide stuffing among peppers, mounding tops. Snugly arrange peppers in single layer in 10- x 10- x 4-inch (5 L) baking dish; top with reserved tops. Mix tomatoes with 1 cup (250 mL) water; spoon around peppers. Tuck bay leaves and basil around edges; drizzle peppers with remaining oil.

Cover with lid or foil; bake in 350°F (180°C) oven until peppers are almost tender, 1 hour. Uncover; bake until tender, 20 minutes.

PER SERVING: about 434 cal, 20 g pro, 18 g total fat (4 g sat. fat), 53 g carb, 5 g fibre, 0 mg chol, 981 mg sodium, 1,039 mg potassium. % RDI: 15% calcium, 35% iron, 28% vit A, 280% vit C, 28% folate.

Tempeh Vegetable Maki Rolls

Prep: 30 minutes **Stand:** 10 minutes **Cook:** 15 minutes **Makes:** 32 pieces

1 pkg (8 oz/240 g) **tempeh,** cut into 6 cubes

1 **green onion,** quartered

4 tsp (20 mL) **sodium-reduced soy sauce**

2 tsp (10 mL) **sesame oil**

2 tsp (10 mL) **rice vinegar** or apple cider vinegar

1½ tsp (7 mL) grated **fresh ginger**

2 tbsp (30 mL) chopped **fresh coriander**

2 tbsp (30 mL) toasted **sesame seeds**

Half large **carrot**

Half **English cucumber,** halved lengthwise and cored

Quarter **sweet red pepper**

1 small **avocado**

Half **lemon**

4 sheets **roasted nori**

1 tbsp (15 mL) **wasabi powder**

✳ Serve these rice-free appetizers with sushi soy sauce or sodium-reduced soy sauce for dipping.

In steamer basket set over pot with 1 inch (2.5 cm) simmering water, steam tempeh and green onion for 15 minutes.

In food processor, purée together tempeh, green onion, soy sauce, sesame oil, vinegar and ginger until smooth. Let cool. Stir in coriander and sesame seeds.

Cut carrot, cucumber and pepper into 8- x ⅛-inch (20 cm x 3 mm) strips. Peel and pit avocado; slice thinly and squeeze lemon juice over top.

Place 1 nori sheet, shiny side down and with long side closest, on bamboo sushi rolling mat. Spread evenly with about one-quarter of the tempeh mixture, leaving ½-inch (1 cm) border along each long side.

Stir wasabi with 2 tsp (10 mL) water; spread one-quarter lengthwise down closest long side of nori, about 2 inches (5 cm) in from edge. Top with one-quarter each of the carrot, cucumber, pepper and avocado.

Using bamboo mat to lift and starting with closest long edge, roll up nori, firmly encasing filling. Set aside, seam side down. Repeat with remaining ingredients to make 4 rolls. Trim ends even. Cut each roll into 8 slices, wiping knife with wet cloth between cuts. (To hold, wrap each in paper towel; set aside for up to 2 hours at room temperature.)

PER PIECE: about 31 cal, 2 g pro, 2 g total fat (trace sat. fat), 2 g carb, 1 g fibre, 0 mg chol, 26 mg sodium, 78 mg potassium. % RDI: 1% calcium, 2% iron, 3% vit A, 5% vit C, 5% folate.

TOFU, TEMPEH & SOY

SEEDS & NUTS

Vegetarian Nut Loaf
(page 161)

From top: Crunchy
Almond Noodle Salad
(opposite), Barley
Mushroom Walnut
Salad (page 58)

Crunchy Almond Noodle Salad

Prep: 12 minutes   **Cook:** 8 minutes   **Makes:** 4 servings

8 oz (250 g) **linguine**

½ cup (125 mL) **natural almond butter**

½ cup (125 mL) **vegetable broth**

¼ cup (60 mL) **soy sauce**

2 tsp (10 mL) **lime** or lemon **juice**

1 clove **garlic,** minced

2 tsp (10 mL) minced **fresh ginger**

Pinch each **salt** and **pepper**

1 large **carrot,** shredded

1 cup (250 mL) **bean sprouts**

Half **sweet red pepper,** thinly sliced

3 **green onions,** thinly sliced

¼ cup (60 mL) chopped toasted **almonds**

In large pot of boiling salted water, cook pasta until al dente, about 8 minutes. Drain and chill under cold water; drain well.

In large bowl, whisk together almond butter, broth, soy sauce, lime juice, garlic, ginger, salt and pepper. Add pasta; toss to coat.

Top with carrot, bean sprouts, red pepper, green onions and almonds. (To store, refrigerate for up to 24 hours.) Toss to combine.

PER SERVING: about 502 cal, 16 g pro, 24 g total fat (2 g sat. fat), 61 g carb, 7 g fibre, 0 mg chol, 1,326 mg sodium. % RDI: 13% calcium, 34% iron, 123% vit A, 65% vit C, 80% folate.

Macadamia Nut Slaw

Prep: 15 minutes   **Makes:** 8 servings

✳ Macadamia nuts are the ideal garnish for this crisp, bright Asian-flavoured slaw. If you don't have any sweet Asian chili sauce on hand, use ½ tsp (2 mL) hot pepper sauce mixed with ¼ tsp (1 mL) granulated sugar.

Quarter head **napa cabbage**
Quarter head **red cabbage**
Half **sweet red pepper**
2 small **carrots**
2 **green onions**
1 **Asian** or Bosc **pear,** peeled and halved
½ cup (125 mL) chopped **macadamia nuts**
3 tbsp (45 mL) chopped **fresh mint**

DRESSING:
¼ cup (60 mL) **vegetable oil**
¼ cup (60 mL) **unseasoned rice vinegar**
4 tsp (20 mL) **lime juice**
2 tsp (10 mL) grated **fresh ginger**
½ tsp (2 mL) **sweet Asian chili sauce**
¼ tsp (1 mL) **salt**

DRESSING: Whisk together oil, vinegar, lime juice, ginger, chili sauce and salt.

Thinly slice napa and red cabbages and red pepper; place in large bowl. Julienne carrots, green onions and pear; add to bowl. Toss with dressing to coat. (To store, cover and refrigerate for up to 6 hours.)

Sprinkle with macadamia nuts and mint.

PER SERVING: about 156 cal, 2 g pro, 14 g total fat (2 g sat. fat), 10 g carb, 3 g fibre, 0 mg chol, 93 mg sodium. % RDI: 5% calcium, 6% iron, 23% vit A, 70% vit C, 19% folate.

Tomato Peanut Soup

Prep: 12 minutes   **Cook:** 30 minutes   **Makes:** 8 servings

* Packed with protein, peanuts give this colourful soup a velvety texture and rich, creamy taste. Our homemade Roasted Vegetable Stock is the most flavourful base for this soup. If you use store-bought vegetable broth instead, combine 3 cups (750 mL) broth with 2 cups (500 mL) water.

1 tbsp (15 mL) **vegetable oil**
1 **onion,** diced
1 stalk **celery,** diced
1 clove **garlic,** minced
1 tsp (5 mL) grated **fresh ginger**
½ tsp (2 mL) **salt**
½ tsp (2 mL) **ground coriander**
Pinch **cayenne pepper**
1 can (28 oz/796 mL) **diced tomatoes**

2 **sweet potatoes** (about 1 lb/ 500 g), peeled and diced
5 cups (1.25 L) **Roasted Vegetable Stock** (page 255)
½ cup (125 mL) **smooth natural peanut butter**
2 cups (500 mL) thinly sliced **kale leaves**
1 tbsp (15 mL) **lemon juice**

In Dutch oven or large saucepan, heat oil over medium heat; fry onion, celery, garlic, ginger, salt, coriander and cayenne, stirring occasionally, until softened, about 3 minutes.

Add tomatoes, sweet potatoes and stock; bring to boil. Whisk in peanut butter; reduce heat and simmer until sweet potatoes are tender, about 20 minutes.

Stir in kale and lemon juice; simmer until kale is wilted, 3 to 5 minutes.

PER SERVING: about 201 cal, 6 g pro, 10 g total fat (1 g sat. fat), 25 g carb, 3 g fibre, 0 mg chol, 922 mg sodium. % RDI: 8% calcium, 12% iron, 108% vit A, 68% vit C, 10% folate.

Roasted Beet & Arugula Salad with Walnut Dressing

Prep: 20 minutes   **Cook:** 1½ hours   **Makes:** 8 servings

1½ lb (750 g) **beets** (6 to 8)

4 cloves **garlic,** sliced

1 sprig **fresh rosemary**

3 tbsp (45 mL) **extra-virgin olive oil**

½ tsp (2 mL) each **salt** and **pepper**

8 cups (2 L) **arugula leaves**

1 cup (250 mL) toasted **walnuts,** coarsely chopped

WALNUT VINAIGRETTE:

⅓ cup (75 mL) **walnut** or extra-virgin olive **oil**

1 small **shallot** (or half green onion), minced

3 tbsp (45 mL) **cider vinegar**

½ tsp (2 mL) **dry mustard**

¼ tsp (1 mL) each **salt** and **pepper**

Pinch **granulated sugar**

Cut off and discard beet greens, leaving 1-inch (2.5 cm) stems attached to beets. Place beets on large piece of foil; sprinkle with garlic, rosemary, oil, salt and pepper. Seal to form packet. Roast on baking sheet in 400°F (200°C) oven until fork-tender, about 1½ hours. Let cool enough to handle.

Peel and trim beets; cut into 1-inch (2.5 cm) thick wedges.

WALNUT VINAIGRETTE: In large bowl, whisk together oil, shallot, vinegar, mustard, salt, pepper and sugar. Transfer 2 tbsp (30 mL) to separate bowl; add beets and toss to coat.

Add arugula to remaining vinaigrette; toss to coat. Divide among plates; top with beets. Sprinkle with walnuts.

PER SERVING: about 254 cal, 3 g pro, 24 g total fat (2 g sat. fat), 10 g carb, 2 g fibre, 0 mg chol, 266 mg sodium. % RDI: 3% calcium, 8% iron, 1% vit A, 5% vit C, 30% folate.

Apple Fennel Celery Salad

Prep: 8 minutes   **Makes:** 6 to 8 servings

1 cup (250 mL) thinly sliced **fennel**

1 cup (250 mL) sliced **celery**

1 cup (250 mL) **red seedless grapes,** halved

2 **Red Delicious apples,** peeled and chopped

½ cup (125 mL) chopped toasted **walnuts**

POPPY SEED DRESSING:

½ cup (125 mL) **Balkan-style plain yogurt**

2 tbsp (30 mL) **liquid honey**

4 tsp (20 mL) **lemon juice**

1 tsp (5 mL) **Dijon mustard**

½ tsp (2 mL) **poppy seeds**

Pinch **salt**

Pinch **paprika**

POPPY SEED DRESSING: In large bowl, whisk together yogurt, honey, lemon juice, mustard, poppy seeds, salt and paprika until smooth.

Add fennel, celery, grapes and apple; toss to coat. Serve sprinkled with walnuts.

PER EACH OF 8 SERVINGS: about 122 cal, 2 g pro, 6 g total fat (1 g sat. fat), 17 g carb, 2 g fibre, 3 mg chol, 36 mg sodium. % RDI: 5% calcium, 4% iron, 2% vit A, 12% vit C, 8% folate.

Brussels Sprouts with Chestnuts & Marsala

Prep: 10 minutes **Cook:** 12 minutes **Makes:** 8 to 10 servings

2 lb (1 kg) **brussels sprouts,** trimmed and halved

3 tbsp (45 mL) **butter**

1 cup (250 mL) **vacuum-packed** or rinsed canned **whole chestnuts,** broken into pieces

⅓ cup (75 mL) **dry Marsala wine**

¼ tsp (1 mL) each **salt** and **pepper**

In large saucepan of boiling salted water, cook brussels sprouts, covered, until tender-crisp, about 6 minutes. Drain.

In Dutch oven, melt butter over medium-high heat; add brussels sprouts, chestnuts, Marsala, salt and pepper. Toss to coat. Boil until heated through and liquid is reduced by half, about 6 minutes.

PER EACH OF 10 SERVINGS: about 110 cal, 3 g pro, 4 g total fat (2 g sat. fat), 16 g carb, 5 g fibre, 9 mg chol, 312 mg sodium. % RDI: 3% calcium, 9% iron, 9% vit A, 98% vit C, 29% folate.

Whipped Sweet Potatoes with Maple Pecan Topping

Prep: 10 minutes   **Cook:** 1¼ hours   **Makes:** 10 to 12 servings

6 **sweet potatoes** (3 lb/1.5 kg), peeled and cubed

2 **russet potatoes** (1 lb/500 g), peeled and cubed

3 **eggs**

2 tbsp (30 mL) **maple syrup**

2 tsp (10 mL) **lemon juice**

¾ tsp (4 mL) **salt**

Pinch **nutmeg**

Pinch **pepper**

1¼ cups (300 mL) chopped **pecans**

⅓ cup (75 mL) packed **brown sugar**

¼ cup (60 mL) **butter,** melted

In large saucepan of boiling salted water, cook sweet and russet potatoes, covered, until tender, about 12 minutes. Drain; return to pot. Mash until smooth.

Beat together eggs, maple syrup, lemon juice, salt, nutmeg and pepper; beat into potatoes. Scrape into greased 13- x 9-inch (3 L) glass baking dish. (To prepare ahead of time, cover and refrigerate for up to 24 hours; add 10 minutes to baking time.)

Stir pecans with brown sugar; sprinkle over potatoes. Drizzle with butter. Bake in 350°F (180°C) oven until set and bubbly, about 50 minutes.

PER EACH OF 12 SERVINGS: about 263 cal, 4 g pro, 13 g total fat (4 g sat. fat), 33 g carb, 4 g fibre, 57 mg chol, 520 mg sodium. % RDI: 5% calcium, 10% iron, 162% vit A, 25% vit C, 8% folate.

SEEDS & NUTS

Shiitake Peanut Pilaf

Prep: 5 minutes **Stand:** 5 minutes **Cook:** 35 minutes **Makes:** 6 servings

2 tbsp (30 mL) **vegetable** or peanut **oil**

⅓ cup (75 mL) **whole raw peanuts** or unsalted roasted peanuts

3 **shallots,** thinly sliced

1½ cups (375 mL) sliced **shiitake mushroom caps**

1 clove **garlic,** minced

Pinch **pepper**

1½ cups (375 mL) **Thai jasmine** or other long-grain **rice**

1 cup (250 mL) **vegetable broth**

1 tsp (5 mL) **sodium-reduced soy sauce**

2 tbsp (30 mL) chopped **fresh coriander**

In saucepan, heat oil over medium heat; fry peanuts, stirring often, until golden, about 4 minutes for raw peanuts, 2 minutes for roasted. With slotted spoon, transfer to paper towel–lined plate.

In same pan, fry shallots, stirring occasionally, until crisp and golden, about 12 minutes.

Add mushrooms, garlic and pepper; cook, stirring, until mushrooms are tender and no liquid remains, about 4 minutes.

Return peanuts to pan. Add rice, stirring to coat. Add broth, soy sauce and 1½ cups (375 mL) water; bring to boil. Reduce heat and simmer, covered, until rice is tender and no liquid remains, about 15 minutes. Let stand, covered, for 5 minutes. Stir in coriander.

PER SERVING: about 266 cal, 7 g pro, 9 g total fat (1 g sat. fat), 41 g carb, 2 g fibre, 1 mg chol, 263 mg sodium. % RDI: 2% calcium, 6% iron, 2% vit A, 10% folate.

Vegetarian Nut Loaf

Prep: 15 minutes **Cook:** 1¼ hours **Makes:** 4 servings

1 tbsp (15 mL) **olive oil**

2 stalks **celery,** diced

1 large **onion,** diced

2 cups (500 mL) finely chopped **white** or cremini **mushrooms**

2 tsp (10 mL) chopped **fresh thyme**

1 tsp (5 mL) **caraway seeds,** ground

½ tsp (2 mL) each **salt** and **pepper**

⅓ cup (75 mL) chopped drained **oil-packed sun-dried tomatoes**

¼ cup (60 mL) **brandy,** sherry or vegetable broth

3 **eggs**

1 cup (250 mL) **fresh whole wheat** or white **bread crumbs**

1 tsp (5 mL) **baking powder**

1 cup (250 mL) chopped **walnuts**

½ cup (125 mL) raw hulled unsalted **sunflower seeds**

½ cup (125 mL) **bottled strained tomatoes** (passata)

* Grind caraway seeds in a spice mill or coffee grinder, in a mortar with pestle, or by crushing on your cutting board using the bottom of a heavy skillet.

In large skillet, heat oil over medium-high heat; sauté celery and onion until softened, about 4 minutes. Stir in mushrooms, thyme, caraway, salt and pepper; sauté until mushrooms are golden, about 4 minutes. Add sun-dried tomatoes and brandy; cook until no liquid remains, about 2 minutes. Let cool.

Beat together eggs, bread crumbs and baking powder; fold in mushroom mixture, walnuts and sunflower seeds. Spread in parchment paper–lined 9- x 5-inch (2 L) loaf pan. Pour strained tomatoes over top.

Bake in 350°F (180°C) oven until slightly puffed and firm, about 1 hour. Let stand for 10 minutes before slicing.

PER SERVING: about 488 cal, 16 g pro, 37 g total fat (5 g sat. fat), 23 g carb, 7 g fibre, 140 mg chol, 570 mg sodium, 679 mg potassium. % RDI: 13% calcium, 32% iron, 8% vit A, 22% vit C, 49% folate.

Wild Rice with Pepitas

Prep: 8 minutes   **Cook:** 1 hour   **Makes:** 8 servings

* If desired, add a handful of dried sour cherries, dried cranberries or chopped dried apricots along with the roasted pepitas. Chilled leftovers make a great salad when tossed with spinach or arugula and a drizzle each of oil and vinegar.

½ cup (125 mL) **pepitas**
1½ cups (375 mL) **wild rice**
1½ tbsp (22 mL) **butter**
1 **onion,** diced

1 **carrot,** finely diced
1 stalk **celery,** finely diced
1 **sweet yellow** or red **pepper,** diced
¾ tsp (4 mL) each **salt** and **pepper**

In dry small skillet, toast pepitas over medium heat until fragrant and starting to pop, about 6 minutes.

In large saucepan of boiling salted water, cook rice, covered, until most of the rice is split and tender, about 45 minutes. Drain in sieve.

In same saucepan, melt butter over medium heat; fry onion, carrot, celery, yellow pepper, salt and pepper, stirring often, until softened, about 7 minutes. Stir in rice; cook until heated through. Stir in pepitas.

PER SERVING: about 192 cal, 6 g pro, 7 g total fat (2 g sat. fat), 29 g carb, 3 g fibre, 7 mg chol, 257 mg sodium. % RDI: 2% calcium, 9% iron, 38% vit A, 50% vit C, 18% folate.

POWERHOUSE PEPITAS

Pepitas, or raw hulled green pumpkin seeds, have long been treasured by native peoples in the United States for their nutrients and medicinal properties. And they are versatile, lending their nutty flavour to salads, snack mixes, cereals, vegetables, rice and pasta dishes, sauces and casseroles. You'll find them year-round in most grocery, bulk food and health food stores.

Curried Lentil Cashew Burgers

Prep: 15 minutes   **Cook:** 30 minutes   **Makes:** 4 servings

½ cup (125 mL) unsalted **cashews**

2 tbsp (30 mL) **vegetable oil**

4 cups (1 L) sliced **white** or cremini **mushrooms**

1 **onion,** chopped

1 clove **garlic,** minced

¼ tsp (1 mL) each **salt** and **pepper**

1 can (19 oz/540 mL) **lentils,** drained and rinsed

1 tbsp (15 mL) **curry paste**

¼ cup (60 mL) **dry bread crumbs**

¼ cup (60 mL) chopped **fresh coriander**

4 slices **Gouda cheese with cumin**

4 leaves **lettuce**

4 slices **red onion**

4 **hamburger buns**

1 **radish** (optional), thinly sliced

In dry skillet, toast cashews over medium-low heat until fragrant, about 5 minutes. Transfer to food processor.

In same skillet, heat 1 tbsp (15 mL) of the oil over medium-high heat; sauté mushrooms, chopped onion, garlic, salt and pepper until no liquid remains, about 5 minutes. Add to food processor.

Add lentils and curry paste to food processor; pulse to combine. Mix in bread crumbs and coriander. Shape into four 1-inch (2.5 cm) thick patties.

In large nonstick skillet, heat remaining oil over medium heat; fry patties until crusty, turning once, about 16 minutes. Top each with cheese slice; cook, covered, until melted, about 1 minute.

Sandwich patties, lettuce, red onion, and radish (if using) in buns.

PER SERVING: about 610 cal, 25 g pro, 27 g total fat (6 g sat. fat), 71 g carb, 10 g fibre, 24 mg chol, 878 mg sodium. % RDI: 27% calcium, 54% iron, 7% vit A, 15% vit C, 131% folate.

SEEDS & NUTS

Vegetable Samosas

Prep: 40 minutes   **Stand:** 30 minutes   **Cook:** 25 minutes   **Makes:** 24 pieces

✳ If you'd rather skip the frying, omit oil for frying and bake the samosas in 425°F (220°C) oven for 15 minutes. Whether fried or baked, they're best freshly made, but for convenience, you can freeze them and reheat later.

2 cups (500 mL) diced peeled **potatoes**

½ cup (125 mL) diced **carrots**

3 tbsp (45 mL) **vegetable oil**

1 tsp (5 mL) **fennel seeds**

1 tsp (5 mL) **cumin seeds**

1 tsp (5 mL) **brown** or black **mustard seeds**

½ tsp (2 mL) **turmeric**

½ tsp (2 mL) **coriander seeds**

½ tsp (2 mL) **fenugreek seeds**

¼ tsp (1 mL) **cayenne pepper**

1 **onion,** chopped

2 cloves **garlic,** minced

1 tbsp (15 mL) grated **fresh ginger**

½ tsp (2 mL) **salt**

½ cup (125 mL) frozen **peas,** thawed

3 tbsp (45 mL) **lemon juice**

2 tbsp (30 mL) chopped **fresh coriander**

Vegetable oil for frying

Fresh Coriander Chutney (page 276)

DOUGH:

2 cups (500 mL) **all-purpose flour**

1 tsp (5 mL) **cumin seeds** (preferably black)

½ tsp (2 mL) **salt**

½ cup (125 mL) **cold butter,** cubed

½ cup (125 mL) **milk**

DOUGH: In food processor or bowl with pastry blender, combine flour, cumin seeds and salt; pulse or cut in butter until in fine crumbs. Pulse or stir in milk until ball begins to form. Press into disc; wrap and refrigerate until chilled, about 30 minutes, or up to 24 hours.

In large saucepan of boiling salted water, cook potatoes and carrots, covered, until tender, about 10 minutes; drain.

Meanwhile, in large skillet, heat oil over medium heat; fry fennel, cumin and mustard seeds, turmeric, coriander and fenugreek seeds, and cayenne just until cumin seeds begin to pop, about 1 minute.

Add onion, garlic, ginger and salt; fry until softened, about 3 minutes. Stir in potato mixture and peas. Stir in lemon juice and coriander; let cool.

Cut dough into 12 pieces; form each into disc. On floured surface, roll out each to 6-inch (15 cm) circle; cut in half. Working with 1 piece at a time, moisten half of the cut edge with water. Form cone shape by overlapping cut edges by ¼ inch (5 mm).

Fill with rounded 1 tbsp (15 mL) of the potato mixture. Moisten top inside edges of pastry; press to seal. Trim jagged edges. Crimp with fork.

In wok or deep saucepan, heat oil to 350°F (180°C) or until 1-inch (2.5 cm) cube of white bread turns golden in 45 seconds.

Fry samosas, in batches, until golden, about 4 minutes. Transfer to paper towel–lined tray. Serve warm with Fresh Coriander Chutney for dipping. (Or, let cool. Refrigerate in airtight container for up to 24 hours. Or freeze on waxed paper–lined tray; transfer to airtight container and freeze for up to 2 weeks. Reheat in 350°F/180°C oven until heated through, 10 to 20 minutes.)

SEEDS & NUTS

PER PIECE: about 133 cal, 2 g pro, 9 g total fat (3 g sat. fat), 12 g carb, 1 g fibre, 12 mg chol, 200 mg sodium. % RDI: 2% calcium, 6% iron, 11% vit A, 5% vit C, 8% folate.

Creamy Walnut Toss

Prep: 5 minutes   **Cook:** 12 minutes   **Makes:** 4 servings

* This quick, robust sauce is just as good with pasta shapes, such as gemelli, farfalle, fusilli or shells (conchiglie), as it is tossed with gnocchi or spooned over polenta.

½ cup (125 mL) chopped **walnuts**

2 tbsp (30 mL) **butter**

2 tsp (10 mL) chopped **fresh thyme**

¾ cup (175 mL) **10% cream**

4 oz (125 g) **Gorgonzola** or other creamy blue cheese, cubed

¼ tsp (1 mL) **pepper**

4 cups (1 L) **short pasta** (12 oz/ 375 g)

2 tbsp (30 mL) chopped **fresh parsley**

In dry Dutch oven or large skillet, toast walnuts over medium heat, stirring often, until fragrant, about 5 minutes.

Add butter and thyme; cook for 30 seconds. Add cream, Gorgonzola cheese and pepper; reduce heat and simmer, stirring occasionally, until slightly thickened and cheese is melted, about 5 minutes.

Meanwhile, in large pot of boiling salted water, cook pasta until al dente, 8 to 10 minutes. Drain well; return to pot. Add sauce; toss to coat. Serve sprinkled with parsley.

PER SERVING: about 620 cal, 21 g pro, 29 g total fat (12 g sat. fat), 69 g carb, 4 g fibre, 51 mg chol, 698 mg sodium. % RDI: 21% calcium, 18% iron, 17% vit A, 3% vit C, 63% folate.

Tofu & Broccoli in Peanut Sauce

Prep: 8 minutes   **Cook:** 6 minutes   **Makes:** 4 servings

1 pkg (425 g) **firm tofu,** drained

¼ cup (60 mL) **natural peanut butter**

2 tbsp (30 mL) **hoisin sauce**

2 tbsp (30 mL) **unseasoned rice vinegar** or cider vinegar

¼ tsp (1 mL) **sriracha,** sambal oelek or hot pepper sauce (optional)

1 tbsp (15 mL) **vegetable oil**

2 **green onions,** chopped

2 cloves **garlic,** minced

3 cups (750 mL) **broccoli florets**

1 **sweet red pepper,** thinly sliced

1 cup (250 mL) **bean sprouts**

¼ cup (60 mL) chopped **fresh coriander**

¼ cup (60 mL) chopped **roasted peanuts**

✳ This dish is packed with protein from the tofu and peanut butter (use smooth or crunchy, depending on your preference). Serve over brown rice or rice noodles.

Pat tofu dry with paper towel; cut into 1-inch (2.5 cm) cubes.

Whisk together ½ cup (125 mL) water, peanut butter, hoisin sauce, vinegar, and sriracha (if using).

In wok or large skillet, heat oil over medium-high heat; stir-fry tofu, green onions and garlic until garlic and tofu are light golden, about 3 minutes.

Add broccoli and red pepper; stir-fry for 1 minute. Add 2 tbsp (30 mL) water; steam, covered, until broccoli is tender-crisp, about 1 minute. Add peanut sauce; cook, stirring, until heated through, about 1 minute. Sprinkle with bean sprouts, coriander and peanuts.

PER SERVING: about 302 cal, 17 g pro, 21 g total fat (3 g sat. fat), 18 g carb, 5 g fibre, 0 mg chol, 192 mg sodium. % RDI: 21% calcium, 23% iron, 16% vit A, 133% vit C, 42% folate.

Chestnut Vegetable Stew
(page 172)

Chestnut Vegetable Stew

Prep: 30 minutes   **Stand:** 10 minutes   **Cook:** 1¼ hours   **Makes:** 8 servings

1 head **garlic**

3 tbsp (45 mL) **olive oil**

1 pkg (10 oz/284 g) **pearl onions,** peeled

1½ lb (750 g) **Yukon Gold potatoes,** peeled and cut into chunks

5 sprigs **fresh parsley**

3 sprigs **fresh thyme**

2 **bay leaves**

1 tsp (5 mL) **salt**

¼ tsp (1 mL) **pepper**

Pinch **saffron**

¼ cup (60 mL) **all-purpose flour**

2 cups (500 mL) **vegetable broth**

Half head **cauliflower,** cut into florets

2 cups (500 mL) **cooked chestnuts** (see Chestnut Know-How, opposite)

1 small **butternut squash** (about 1½ lb/750 g), peeled, seeded and cut into chunks

Trim top off garlic to expose cloves. Place on piece of foil; drizzle with 1 tsp (5 mL) of the oil. Seal to form packet. Bake in 375°F (190°C) oven until tender, about 35 minutes. Let cool enough to handle; squeeze out cloves into bowl.

Meanwhile, in large Dutch oven, heat remaining oil over medium heat; fry onions, stirring occasionally, until golden, about 6 minutes.

Stir in potatoes, parsley and thyme sprigs, bay leaves, salt, pepper, saffron and roasted garlic; cook, stirring, for 2 minutes.

Stir in flour; cook, stirring, for 2 minutes. Gradually stir in broth, scraping up brown bits from bottom of pan. Stir in 3 cups (750 mL) water; bring to boil. Reduce heat and simmer, covered, for 10 minutes.

Stir in cauliflower and chestnuts; simmer for 5 minutes. Stir in squash; simmer until tender, about 15 minutes. Discard parsley, thyme and bay leaves.

PER SERVING: about 263 cal, 5 g pro, 6 g total fat (1 g sat. fat), 50 g carb, 8 g fibre, 1 mg chol, 492 mg sodium, 751 mg potassium. % RDI: 6% calcium, 11% iron, 79% vit A, 72% vit C, 33% folate.

CHESTNUT KNOW-HOW

• If available, fresh chestnuts have the best flavour. To prepare, carefully cut an X in flat side of each. Boil, 4 at a time, until cut points curl, about 2 minutes. Drain and peel off skin. Then simmer in fresh water until tender, about 5 minutes.

• Vacuum-packed or canned chestnuts, available in some grocery stores and specialty food shops, are convenient and ready-to-use. Of the two types, vacuum-packed have a superior taste. Drain and rinse canned chestnuts before using.

Chestnut Tourtière

Prep: 20 minutes   **Stand:** 30 minutes   **Cook:** 50 minutes   **Makes:** 12 servings

✳ This savoury, hearty holiday-time pie is best served with chili sauce or Winter Fruit Chutney (page 277).

1 lb (500 g) **cremini** or white **mushrooms**

¼ cup (60 mL) **butter**

1 **onion,** finely chopped

2 **carrots,** finely diced

1 inner stalk **celery** with leaves, finely diced

1 tsp (5 mL) **salt**

1 tsp (5 mL) **dried savory**

½ tsp (2 mL) **ground allspice**

¼ tsp (1 mL) **mace**

¼ tsp (1 mL) **pepper**

Pinch **ground cloves**

¼ cup (60 mL) **brandy** or vegetable broth

⅓ cup (75 mL) chopped **fresh parsley**

1 **egg,** beaten

3 cups (750 mL) **cooked chestnuts** (see Chestnut Know-How, page 173)

2 tbsp (30 mL) **whipping cream** or milk

PASTRY:

2½ cups (625 mL) **all-purpose flour**

½ tsp (2 mL) **salt**

¾ cup (175 mL) cold **unsalted butter,** cubed

2 **egg yolks**

6 tbsp (90 mL) **cold water** (approx)

PASTRY: In food processor or bowl, pulse or stir flour with salt; pulse or cut in butter until in fine crumbs with a few larger pieces. Pulse in egg yolks just until combined. Pulse in just enough water for dough to hold together when pressed. Gently pat together; divide in half and press into discs. Wrap each and refrigerate until chilled, about 30 minutes, or for up to 2 days.

Meanwhile, break mushrooms into pieces; finely chop in food processor.

In skillet, heat butter over medium heat; fry onion, stirring occasionally, until golden, about 5 minutes. Add carrots and celery; cook, stirring, for 2 minutes.

Add mushrooms, salt, savory, allspice, mace, pepper and cloves; cook until liquid is released from mushrooms, about 10 minutes. Add brandy; cook over medium-high heat until no liquid remains, about 1 minute. Transfer to bowl; let cool.

Stir in parsley and egg. With fork, mash 1 cup (250 mL) of the chestnuts until crumbly; mix into mushroom mixture. Stir in remaining chestnuts.

On lightly floured surface, roll out each pastry disc to 12-inch (30 cm) circle. Fit 1 into 10-inch (25 cm) pie plate; trim overhang even with rim. Spoon in filling. Lightly brush rim with water; top with remaining pastry. Trim edge; flute or use fork to seal. Brush with cream; cut steam vents in top.

Bake in bottom third of 425°F (220°C) oven until golden, about 40 minutes. Let stand for 10 minutes before slicing.

PER SERVING: about 362 cal, 6 g pro, 19 g total fat (11 g sat. fat), 42 g carb, 7 g fibre, 93 mg chol, 337 mg sodium. % RDI: 4% calcium, 14% iron, 39% vit A, 20% vit C, 43% folate.

EGGS & CHEESE

Ricotta Tartlets & Salad
with Tarragon Vinaigrette
(page 180)

Cheddar & Leek Soup

Prep: 8 minutes **Cook:** 40 minutes **Makes:** 8 servings

¼ cup (60 mL) **butter**

1 bunch **leeks** (white and light green parts only), chopped

1 large **onion,** chopped

⅓ cup (75 mL) **all-purpose flour**

3 cups (750 mL) **vegetable broth**

1 can (440 mL) **English-style ale**

¼ tsp (1 mL) **salt**

½ cup (125 mL) **whipping cream**

12 oz (375 g) **old Cheddar cheese,** shredded (about 4 cups/1 L)

2 tsp (10 mL) **hot mustard**

½ tsp (2 mL) **Worcestershire sauce**

¼ tsp (1 mL) **pepper**

In large saucepan or Dutch oven, melt butter over medium heat; fry leeks and onion, stirring often, until softened, about 5 minutes.

Add flour; cook, stirring, just until starting to brown, about 2 minutes. Slowly stir in broth, 2 cups (500 mL) water, ale and salt; bring to simmer. Reduce heat to low; simmer, covered, for 30 minutes.

Stir in cream; bring just to boil over medium heat. Stir in cheese, mustard, Worcestershire sauce and pepper; reduce heat to low. Stir until cheese is melted.

* This rich and intensely flavoured English-style soup will become a cold weather favourite. Use a three- to five-year-old Cheddar for the best flavour. At the end of cooking, adjust salt to taste if necessary, because the salt contents of the cheese and broth vary. Pass the pepper mill at the table.

EGGS & CHEESE

PER SERVING: about 331 cal, 13 g pro, 25 g total fat (16 g sat. fat), 14 g carb, 1 g fibre, 80 mg chol, 915 mg sodium, 146 mg potassium. % RDI: 32% calcium, 8% iron, 23% vit A, 3% vit C, 15% folate.

Ricotta Tartlets & Salad with Tarragon Vinaigrette

Prep: 10 minutes   **Cook:** 20 minutes.   **Makes:** 6 servings

✳ Soufflé-like tartlets add a lovely French element to this elegant herbed salad. They could also be bases for canapés or floated in bowls of creamy soup.

½ cup (125 mL) finely grated **Parmesan cheese**

1 cup (250 mL) **ricotta cheese**

1 **egg white**

1 tbsp (15 mL) chopped **fresh thyme**

1 tbsp (15 mL) **all-purpose flour**

¼ tsp (1 mL) **pepper**

¼ tsp (1 mL) **baking powder**

¼ tsp (1 mL) crumbled **dried lavender** (optional)

SALAD:

1 tbsp (15 mL) **tarragon vinegar** or white wine vinegar

1 tsp (5 mL) **Dijon mustard**

¼ tsp (1 mL) crumbled **dried savory**

Pinch each **salt** and **pepper**

¼ cup (60 mL) **extra-virgin olive oil**

8 cups (2 L) **mixed baby salad greens**

¼ cup (60 mL) finely chopped **fresh chives** or green onions

Grease 12 mini-muffin cups; sprinkle sides and bottoms with 2 tbsp (30 mL) of the Parmesan cheese to coat.

Beat together ricotta, egg white, remaining Parmesan cheese, thyme, flour, pepper, baking powder, and lavender (if using) until smooth. Spoon evenly into prepared muffin cups.

Bake in centre of 350°F (180°C) oven until puffed and tester inserted in centre comes out clean, about 20 minutes. Let cool in pan on rack for 5 minutes.

SALAD: In large bowl, whisk together vinegar, mustard, savory, salt and pepper; gradually whisk in oil. Add salad greens and chives; toss to coat. Divide among 6 plates; top each with 2 tartlets.

PER SERVING: about 209 cal, 10 g pro, 17 g total fat (6 g sat. fat), 5 g carb, 1 g fibre, 28 mg chol, 212 mg sodium. % RDI: 22% calcium, 8% iron, 23% vit A, 20% vit C, 32% folate.

Seared Halloumi Salad

Prep: 10 minutes   **Cook:** 5 minutes   **Makes:** 4 servings

8 oz (250 g) **halloumi cheese**

¼ cup (60 mL) **all-purpose flour**

¼ cup (60 mL) **extra-virgin olive oil**

1 tbsp (15 mL) **red wine vinegar**

¼ tsp (1 mL) **dried oregano**

Pinch each **salt** and **pepper**

6 cups (1.5 L) torn **mixed salad greens**

4 tsp (20 mL) chopped **fresh mint**

½ cup (125 mL) thinly sliced **cucumber**

16 pitted **black olives,** such as Kalamata

16 **grape** or cherry **tomatoes,** halved

*Halloumi is a firm, mild cheese that holds its shape well when cooked. You'll find it in some specialty cheese shops and supermarkets, or at Cypriot or other Mediterranean grocery stores.

181

Cut halloumi into ¼-inch (5 mm) thick slices; coat in flour, brushing off excess.

Whisk together 3 tbsp (45 mL) of the oil, vinegar, oregano, salt and pepper.

Toss salad greens with mint; arrange on plates. Top with cucumber, olives and tomatoes.

In large nonstick skillet, heat remaining oil over medium-high heat; fry halloumi, turning once, until deep golden, about 4 minutes. Arrange on salad; drizzle with dressing.

PER SERVING: about 383 cal, 15 g pro, 33 g total fat (13 g sat. fat), 9 g carb, 3 g fibre, 38 mg chol, 612 mg sodium. % RDI: 19% calcium, 18% iron, 46% vit A, 35% vit C, 41% folate.

Chef's Salad

Prep: 12 minutes   **Makes:** 4 servings

✳ To hard-cook eggs, place eggs in saucepan; cover with cold water and bring to boil. Remove from heat and let stand, covered, for 20 minutes. Drain; rinse under cold water until cool enough to handle. Peel off shells.

6 cups (1.5 L) torn **iceberg lettuce** (about half head)

2 cups (500 mL) torn **radicchio** (about half head)

4 **radishes,** thinly sliced

¾ cup (175 mL) sliced **cucumber**

½ cup (125 mL) **alfalfa sprouts** (about half 35 g pkg)

⅓ cup (75 mL) thinly sliced **sweet onion**

½ cup (125 mL) rinsed drained **canned chickpeas**

3 **hard-cooked eggs,** quartered

1 large **tomato,** cut into 12 wedges

Half **avocado,** peeled and sliced

2 oz (60 g) **Swiss cheese,** cut into batonnets

2 oz (60 g) **Cheddar cheese,** cut into batonnets

DRESSING:

¼ cup (60 mL) **light mayonnaise**

1 tbsp (15 mL) minced **dill pickle**

1 tbsp (15 mL) **extra-virgin olive oil**

2 tsp (10 mL) **chili sauce**

1½ tsp (7 mL) **lemon juice**

½ tsp (2 mL) drained **capers,** minced

½ tsp (2 mL) **Dijon mustard**

Pinch each **salt** and **pepper**

DRESSING: Stir together mayonnaise, pickle, oil, chili sauce, lemon juice, capers, mustard, salt and pepper.

Toss together lettuce, radicchio, radishes, cucumber, sprouts, onion and half of the Dressing; arrange on 4 large plates.

Top with chickpeas, eggs, tomato, avocado and Swiss and Cheddar cheeses; spoon remaining dressing over top.

PER SERVING: about 349 cal, 16 g pro, 25 g total fat (9 g sat. fat), 17 g carb, 5 g fibre, 173 mg chol, 430 mg sodium. % RDI: 25% calcium, 14% iron, 20% vit A, 32% vit C, 60% folate.

Potato Salad Niçoise

Prep: 8 minutes   **Cook:** 14 minutes   **Makes:** 4 servings

14 mini **new potatoes,** quartered (1 lb/500 g)

2 cups (500 mL) trimmed **green beans**

3 tbsp (45 mL) **extra-virgin olive oil**

3 tbsp (45 mL) **lemon juice**

1 tsp (5 mL) **Dijon mustard**

½ tsp (2 mL) **dried basil**

½ tsp (2 mL) **salt**

¼ tsp (1 mL) **pepper**

2 cups (500 mL) **baby spinach,** trimmed

1 cup (250 mL) **grape tomatoes,** halved

16 **oil-cured black olives,** pitted

Half **sweet red pepper,** diced

4 **hard-cooked eggs,** quartered

In large pot of boiling salted water, cook potatoes, covered, until almost tender, about 10 minutes.

Add green beans; cook until tender-crisp, about 4 minutes. Drain.

In large bowl, whisk together oil, lemon juice, mustard, basil, salt and pepper. Add potato mixture, spinach, tomatoes, olives and red pepper; toss to coat. Top with eggs.

PER SERVING: about 336 cal, 10 g pro, 22 g total fat (3 g sat. fat), 28 g carb, 5 g fibre, 186 mg chol, 1,282 mg sodium. % RDI: 10% calcium, 22% iron, 41% vit A, 102% vit C, 51% folate.

Toasted Guacamole, Brie & Tomato Sandwiches

Prep: 10 minutes   **Cook:** 8 minutes   **Makes:** 4 servings

✳ These gourmet grilled cheese sandwiches could also be made in a panini press. Switch up the bread with multigrain, sun-dried tomato, herbed or black olive bread if desired.

EGGS & CHEESE

3 tbsp (45 mL) **butter,** softened

8 thick slices country-style **white bread**

2 **tomatoes,** thinly sliced

4 oz (125 g) **Brie cheese,** sliced

GUACAMOLE:

1 **avocado**

2 **green onions,** thinly sliced

2 cloves **garlic,** minced

1 tbsp (15 mL) **lemon juice**

2 tsp (10 mL) **extra-virgin olive oil**

½ tsp (2 mL) **hot pepper sauce**

¼ tsp (1 mL) each **salt** and **pepper**

GUACAMOLE: Halve and pit avocado; scoop flesh into bowl and mash. Mix in green onions, garlic, lemon juice, oil, hot pepper sauce, salt and pepper.

Butter 1 side of each bread slice; spread guacamole on opposite side of 4 of the slices. Arrange 4 slices, butter side down, in large skillet; top each with tomatoes and cheese. Top with remaining bread, butter side up.

Cook over medium heat, pressing and turning once, until golden and crisp, and cheese is melted, about 8 minutes.

PER SERVING: about 531 cal, 15 g pro, 30 g total fat (12 g sat. fat), 53 g carb, 6 g fibre, 56 mg chol, 911 mg sodium. % RDI: 15% calcium, 28% iron, 20% vit A, 32% vit C, 68% folate.

Mushroom Fontina Pizza

Prep: 12 minutes **Cook:** 40 minutes **Makes:** 8 slices

1 lb (500 g) **white** or cremini **mushrooms,** stemmed

1 tbsp (15 mL) **extra-virgin olive oil**

1 small **onion,** minced

2 cloves **garlic,** minced

¼ tsp (1 mL) each **salt** and **pepper**

2 tbsp (30 mL) chopped **fresh parsley**

1⅓ to 1½ lb (680 to 750 g) **whole wheat pizza dough,** at room temperature, or Multigrain Pizza Dough (page 267)

2 tbsp (30 mL) chopped **fresh thyme**

1½ cups (375 mL) shredded **Fontina cheese**

In food processor, pulse mushrooms until coarse paste.

In skillet, heat oil over medium heat; fry onion, garlic, salt and pepper, stirring occasionally, until onion is softened, about 5 minutes.

Stir in mushroom paste; cook, stirring, until no liquid remains, about 15 minutes. Stir in parsley.

On lightly floured surface, stretch or roll out dough to 14-inch (35 cm) circle; transfer to greased pizza pan. Spread with mushroom mixture, sprinkle with thyme and Fontina cheese.

Bake in bottom third of 425°F (220°C) oven until bottom is golden and cheese is bubbly, about 20 minutes.

✳ The earthy flavour of the mushrooms and the creamy, nutty flavour of Fontina work beautifully with the multigrain dough. For added flavour, drizzle with truffle or porcini oil before serving.

EGGS & CHEESE

PER SLICE: about 351 cal, 15 g pro, 14 g total fat (5 g sat. fat), 44 g carb, 5 g fibre, 25 mg chol, 533 mg sodium. % RDI: 14% calcium, 28% iron, 7% vit A, 8% vit C, 42% folate.

Onion & Gorgonzola Pizza with Arugula

Prep: 10 minutes   **Cook:** 30 minutes   **Makes:** 8 slices

2 tbsp (30 mL) **extra-virgin olive oil**

1 large **sweet onion,** chopped

¼ tsp (1 mL) each **salt** and **pepper**

1⅓ to 1½ lb (680 to 750 g) **pizza dough,** at room temperature, or Pizza Dough (page 268)

1 tbsp (15 mL) **cornmeal**

4 oz (125 g) **Gorgonzola cheese,** thinly sliced or crumbled

⅓ cup (75 mL) grated **Parmesan cheese**

2 cups (500 mL) lightly packed trimmed **baby arugula**

In skillet, heat oil over medium heat; fry onion, salt and pepper, stirring occasionally, until onion is softened, about 7 minutes. Let cool slightly.

On lightly floured surface, stretch or roll out dough to 14-inch (35 cm) circle. (Or into 16- x 12-inch/40 x 30 cm rectangle.)

Sprinkle cornmeal evenly over pizza pan or baking sheet; lay dough in pan. Spread with onion mixture; top with Gorgonzola cheese. Sprinkle with Parmesan cheese.

Bake in bottom third of 425°F (220°C) oven until bottom is golden, 20 to 25 minutes. Transfer to cutting board; top with arugula.

PER SLICE: about 333 cal, 11 g pro, 13 g total fat (4 g sat. fat), 42 g carb, 3 g fibre, 18 mg chol, 792 mg sodium. % RDI: 24% calcium, 20% iron, 8% vit A, 7% vit C, 45% folate.

Pizza Margherita

Prep: 10 minutes   **Cook:** 16 minutes   **Makes:** 4 slices

1 to 1⅓ lb (500 to 680 g) **pizza dough,** at room temperature, or Pizza Dough (page 268)

1 can (28 oz/796 mL) **whole tomatoes,** drained, seeded and chopped

¼ tsp (1 mL) **salt**

3 tbsp (45 mL) **extra-virgin olive oil**

5 oz (150 g) **mozzarella ball,** thinly sliced into about 8 pieces

8 **Kalamata** or oil-cured **black olives,** halved

8 to 10 **fresh basil leaves**

On lightly floured surface, stretch or roll out dough to 12-inch (30 cm) circle; transfer to greased pizza pan.

Spread tomatoes over dough; sprinkle with salt. Drizzle with 2 tbsp (30 mL) of the oil; arrange cheese and olives over top.

Bake in bottom third of 475°F (240°C) oven until bottom is golden and cheese is bubbly, 16 to 18 minutes.

Sprinkle with basil leaves; drizzle with remaining oil.

EGGS & CHEESE

PER SLICE: about 475 cal, 15 g pro, 23 g total fat (7 g sat. fat), 51 g carb, 2 g fibre, 32 mg chol, 918 mg sodium, 321 mg potassium. % RDI: 23% calcium, 31% iron, 9% vit A, 23% vit C, 74% folate.

Black Bean & Scrambled Egg Enchiladas

Prep: 20 minutes   **Cook:** 55 minutes   **Makes:** 8 servings

1 can (19 oz/540 mL) **black beans,** drained and rinsed

1 can (4½ oz/127 mL) chopped **green chilies,** drained

1 tbsp (15 mL) **lime juice**

12 **eggs**

3 **green onions,** thinly sliced

¼ tsp (1 mL) each **salt** and **pepper**

2 tbsp (30 mL) **butter**

8 large (10-inch/25 cm) **flour tortillas**

¾ cup (175 mL) shredded **Monterey Jack** or old Cheddar cheese

ENCHILADA SAUCE:

1 tbsp (15 mL) **olive oil**

1 **red onion,** diced

1 clove **garlic,** minced

1 bottle (680 mL) **strained tomatoes** (passata)

1 cup (250 mL) **vegetable broth**

2 tsp (10 mL) **chili powder**

1 tsp (5 mL) **dried oregano**

¼ tsp (1 mL) **salt**

¼ cup (60 mL) chopped **fresh coriander**

ENCHILADA SAUCE: In saucepan, heat oil over medium heat; fry onion and garlic until onion is softened, about 3 minutes. Stir in tomatoes, broth, chili powder, oregano and salt; bring to boil. Reduce heat and simmer for 15 minutes. Stir in coriander.

Combine beans, chilies, lime juice and ½ cup (125 mL) of the Enchilada Sauce; mash with fork until chunky. Beat together eggs, ¼ cup (60 mL) water, half of the green onions, the salt and pepper. In skillet, melt butter over medium heat; cook eggs, stirring, just until softly set but still moist, about 5 minutes.

Divide bean mixture among tortillas, spreading evenly. Spoon egg mixture along bottom third of each; roll up tortillas. Arrange in single layer, seam side down, in greased 13- x 9-inch (3 L) glass baking dish. Spoon 3 cups (750 mL) of the remaining Enchilada Sauce over top. Sprinkle with cheese and remaining green onions.

Bake in 375°F (190°C) oven until bubbly, about 30 minutes. Serve with remaining sauce.

PER SERVING: about 517 cal, 22 g pro, 21 g total fat (8 g sat. fat), 59 g carb, 7 g fibre, 297 mg chol, 1,138 mg sodium, 439 mg potassium. % RDI: 17% calcium, 44% iron, 19% vit A, 12% vit C, 77% folate.

Mushroom
Fried Rice Omelettes

Prep: 12 minutes   **Cook:** 20 minutes   **Makes:** 4 servings

3 tbsp (45 mL) **vegetable oil**

1 **onion,** diced

1 **carrot,** diced

1 cup (250 mL) chopped **cremini mushrooms**

1 cup (250 mL) **frozen peas,** thawed

½ tsp (2 mL) each **salt** and **pepper**

3 cups (750 mL) cold **cooked rice**

3 tbsp (45 mL) **ketchup**

1 tbsp (15 mL) **sodium-reduced soy sauce**

3 **green onions,** chopped

8 **eggs**

4 tsp (20 mL) **butter**

In wok or large nonstick skillet, heat oil over medium-high heat; stir-fry onion and carrot until almost tender, 2 to 3 minutes.

Add mushrooms; stir-fry for 1 minute. Add peas; stir-fry until hot. Add half each of the salt and pepper.

Stir in rice, ketchup and soy sauce; stir-fry until hot. Sprinkle with green onions. Keep warm.

Whisk together eggs, remaining salt and pepper, and 2 tbsp (30 mL) water just until blended but not frothy.

In 8-inch (20 cm) nonstick skillet, melt 1 tsp (5 mL) of the butter over medium heat. Add one-quarter of the egg mixture. Cook, gently lifting edge with spatula to allow uncooked eggs to flow underneath, until set, 3 to 4 minutes. Slide onto plate.

Spoon one-quarter of the rice mixture over half of omelette; fold uncovered half over filling. Repeat with remaining ingredients to make 3 more omelettes.

PER SERVING: about 533 cal, 19 g pro, 25 g total fat (6 g sat. fat), 58 g carb, 4 g fibre, 382 mg chol, 748 mg sodium. % RDI: 9% calcium, 18% iron, 58% vit A, 12% vit C, 40% folate.

Asparagus Goat Cheese Omelettes

Prep: 10 minutes   **Cook:** 20 minutes   **Makes:** 4 servings

8 **eggs**

¼ tsp (1 mL) each **salt** and **pepper**

4 tsp (20 mL) **butter**

FILLING:

1 bunch **asparagus**
   (about 1 lb/500 g)

1 tbsp (15 mL) **olive oil**

3 **green onions,** sliced

1 tbsp (15 mL) chopped **fresh tarragon**

4 oz (125 g) **goat cheese,** crumbled

FILLING: Snap off woody ends of asparagus. In large skillet, heat oil over medium heat; cook asparagus and green onions, stirring occasionally, until tender, about 3 minutes. Stir in tarragon; cook for 1 minute. Transfer to bowl.

In separate bowl, whisk together eggs, salt, pepper and 2 tbsp (30 mL) water just until blended but not frothy.

In 8-inch (20 cm) nonstick skillet, melt 1 tsp (5 mL) of the butter over medium heat. Add one-quarter of the egg mixture; cook, gently lifting edge with spatula to allow uncooked eggs to flow underneath, until almost set, 2 to 3 minutes.

Place one-quarter of the vegetable mixture over half of omelette; sprinkle with one-quarter of the cheese. Fold uncovered half over filling; cook for 1 minute. Slide onto plate. Repeat with remaining ingredients to make 3 more omelettes.

PER SERVING: about 306 cal, 20 g pro, 23 g total fat (10 g sat. fat), 5 g carb, 2 g fibre, 395 mg chol, 410 mg sodium, 346 mg potassium. % RDI: 11% calcium, 19% iron, 35% vit A, 12% vit C, 80% folate.

Spanish Tortilla

Prep: 5 minutes   **Stand:** 3 minutes   **Cook:** 45 minutes   **Makes:** 6 servings

2 **Yukon Gold potatoes**
  (about 1 lb/500 g)
3 tbsp (45 mL) **vegetable oil**
2 **onions,** thinly sliced
2 cloves **garlic,** minced

½ tsp (2 mL) **salt**
¼ tsp (1 mL) **pepper**
Pinch **cayenne pepper**
6 **eggs,** beaten

✳ Serve warm or at room temperature, sprinkled with chopped fresh mint or parsley if desired. To ovenproof a skillet, wrap the handle in heavy-duty foil.

Peel potatoes. Cut in half lengthwise; thinly slice crosswise.

In 10-inch (25 cm) ovenproof nonstick skillet, heat oil over medium heat; fry potatoes, onions, garlic, salt, pepper and cayenne, stirring occasionally, until potatoes are tender and onions are light golden, about 20 minutes.

Smooth top. Pour eggs over potato mixture; cook over medium-low heat until set around edge, about 20 minutes.

Broil, about 6 inches (15 cm) from heat, until golden and eggs are completely set, about 2 minutes. Loosen edge. Let stand for 3 minutes.

Invert onto plate; invert again onto another plate so top is up. Let stand for 5 minutes before cutting into wedges. (Or, let cool for 30 minutes; refrigerate in airtight container for up to 2 days.)

EGGS & CHEESE

PER SERVING: about 201 cal, 8 g pro, 12 g total fat (3 g sat. fat), 16 g carb, 1 g fibre, 187 mg chol, 256 mg sodium. % RDI: 4% calcium, 5% iron, 7% vit A, 9% vit C, 16% folate.

Singapore Rice Crêpes with Scrambled Eggs & Curried Vegetables

Prep: 10 minutes   **Stand:** 30 minutes   **Cook:** 25 minutes   **Makes:** 6 servings

✳ Before rolling these up, if desired, garnish with crushed dry roasted peanuts; sliced hot peppers or hot pepper sauce; fresh lime juice; and sprigs of fresh coriander, basil or mint.

1 cup (250 mL) **rice flour**
4 tsp (20 mL) **all-purpose flour**
¼ tsp (1 mL) **salt**
3 **eggs**
1 tsp (5 mL) **vegetable oil**

CURRIED VEGETABLES:
1 tbsp (15 mL) **vegetable oil**
1 **onion,** thinly sliced
3 cloves **garlic,** minced
1 **carrot,** julienned

1 cup (250 mL) **snow peas,** julienned
4 tsp (20 mL) **mild curry paste**
2 cups (500 mL) **bean sprouts**
1 tbsp (15 mL) **soy sauce**

SCRAMBLED EGGS:
8 **eggs**
¼ tsp (1 mL) each **salt** and **pepper**
1 tbsp (15 mL) **butter**

Whisk together rice flour, all-purpose flour and salt. Whisk together eggs, 1½ cups (375 mL) water and oil; pour over flour mixture and stir until combined. Let stand for 30 minutes.

Heat greased 8-inch (20 cm) nonstick skillet over medium heat. Stirring batter each time, pour scant ¼ cup (60 mL) into pan for each crêpe, swirling to coat; cook until top is dry, 1 to 2 minutes. Stack on plate; cover with damp tea towel. (To store, let cool; refrigerate in airtight container for up to 1 day.)

CURRIED VEGETABLES: In nonstick skillet, heat oil over medium heat; fry onion, stirring occasionally, until golden, about 8 minutes. Add garlic, carrot, snow peas and curry paste; cook, stirring occasionally, until vegetables are tender-crisp, about 5 minutes. Add bean sprouts and soy sauce; cook, stirring, just until sprouts are slightly wilted, about 1 minute.

SCRAMBLED EGGS: Whisk together eggs, salt and pepper. In skillet, melt butter over medium heat; cook eggs, stirring, just until softly set but still moist, about 4 minutes.

Spoon some of the Curried Vegetables down centre of each crêpe; top with Scrambled Eggs. Roll up.

PER SERVING: about 331 cal, 15 g pro, 16 g total fat (5 g sat. fat), 31 g carb, 2 g fibre, 512 mg sodium. % RDI: 7% calcium, 17% iron, 50% vit A, 18% vit C, 26% folate.

Corn & Leek Quiche

Prep: 20 minutes   **Stand:** 1¾ hours   **Cook:** 1¼ hours   **Makes:** 8 servings

1 tbsp (15 mL) **olive oil**

2 **leeks** (white and light green parts only), thinly sliced

1 cup (250 mL) **fresh corn kernels**

2 tsp (10 mL) chopped **fresh thyme**

½ tsp (2 mL) **pepper**

¼ tsp (1 mL) **salt**

½ cup (125 mL) shredded **Gruyère cheese**

4 **eggs**

¾ cup (175 mL) **5% cream**

CORNMEAL PASTRY:

1¼ cups (300 mL) **all-purpose flour**

¼ cup (60 mL) **cornmeal**

½ tsp (2 mL) **granulated sugar**

½ tsp (2 mL) **salt**

½ cup (125 mL) cold **unsalted butter**, cubed

3 tbsp (45 mL) **sour cream**

2 tbsp (30 mL) **ice water** (approx)

CORNMEAL PASTRY: Mix flour, cornmeal, sugar and salt; using pastry blender or 2 knives, cut in butter until in large crumbs. Whisk sour cream with water; drizzle over flour mixture, tossing with fork until dough comes together and adding up to 1 tbsp (15 mL) more water if necessary. Wrap and refrigerate until chilled, 1 hour, or up to 24 hours.

On lightly floured surface, roll out pastry to scant ¼-inch (**5 mm**) thickness; fit into 9-inch (23 cm) quiche dish or pie plate. Fold overhang under, leaving ¼ inch (5 mm) above rim; flute or crimp edge with fork. Prick all over with fork. Refrigerate for 30 minutes.

Line pie shell with foil; fill with pie weights or dried beans. Bake in bottom third of 400°F (200°C) oven until rim is light golden, 20 minutes. Remove weights and foil; bake for 10 minutes. Let cool on rack.

Meanwhile, in large skillet, heat oil over medium heat; fry leeks, corn, thyme, pepper and salt over medium heat, stirring, until leeks are softened, 5 minutes. Sprinkle cheese over pastry shell. Whisk eggs with cream; stir in corn mixture. Pour into crust. Shielding pastry rim with foil, bake in centre of 375°F (190°C) oven until knife inserted in centre comes out clean, 40 minutes. Let cool in pan on rack for 10 minutes before serving. (Or, let cool for 30 minutes; cover and refrigerate for up to 24 hours. Reheat in 350°F/180°C oven for 20 minutes.)

PER SERVING: about 375 cal, 9 g pro, 20 g total fat (11 g sat. fat), 39 g carb, 2 g fibre, 141 mg chol, 299 mg sodium, 145 mg potassium. % RDI: 13% calcium, 13% iron, 17% vit A, 5% vit C, 35% folate.

Golden Buck Welsh Rarebit

Prep: 10 minutes **Cook:** 16 minutes **Makes:** 4 servings

½ cup (125 mL) full-bodied **beer,** such as dark ale or porter

1½ cups (375 mL) shredded **old Cheddar cheese**

2 **eggs,** lightly beaten

2 tsp (10 mL) **Dijon mustard**

¼ tsp (1 mL) each **salt** and **pepper**

¼ tsp (1 mL) **Worcestershire sauce**

4 thick slices **whole wheat bread,** toasted

1 tsp (5 mL) **vinegar**

4 **eggs**

Pinch **cayenne pepper**

In saucepan, bring beer to simmer over medium heat; stir in cheese until melted. Whisk in beaten eggs, mustard, salt, pepper and Worcestershire sauce; cook until thick enough to coat back of spoon, about 2 minutes.

Place toast on parchment paper–lined baking sheet; pour cheese mixture over each. Broil, watching closely, until cheese is golden, about 2 minutes.

Meanwhile, in shallow saucepan, bring 3 inches (8 cm) water to boil. Add vinegar; reduce heat to simmer. One at a time, break eggs into dish and gently slip into water; cook until whites are set and yolks are still liquid, 3 to 5 minutes. With slotted spoon, remove; drain well. Spoon 1 onto each toast; sprinkle with cayenne.

PER SERVING: about 399 cal, 24 g pro, 23 g total fat (12 g sat. fat), 24 g carb, 4 g fibre, 367 mg chol, 767 mg sodium. % RDI: 35% calcium, 20% iron, 27% vit A, 25% folate.

Herb Goat Cheese Soufflé with Roasted Cherry Tomatoes

Prep: 12 minutes   **Cook:** 30 minutes   **Makes:** 4 servings

8 **eggs,** separated

1 cup (250 mL) **milk**

3 tbsp (45 mL) **all-purpose flour**

2 tbsp (30 mL) minced **fresh parsley**

½ tsp (2 mL) **salt**

Pinch **pepper**

Pinch **cayenne pepper**

1 pkg (4½ oz/140 g) **goat cheese**

ROASTED CHERRY TOMATOES:

4 cups (1 L) **cherry** or grape **tomatoes,** halved

2 tbsp (30 mL) **extra-virgin olive oil**

1 tbsp (15 mL) **balsamic vinegar**

½ tsp (2 mL) **salt**

8 **fresh basil leaves,** thinly sliced

ROASTED CHERRY TOMATOES: In 13- x 9-inch (3 L) glass baking dish, toss together tomatoes, oil, vinegar and salt.

Whisk together egg yolks, milk, flour, parsley, salt, pepper and cayenne. Crumble goat cheese into egg mixture; whisk until combined but still slightly lumpy.

Beat egg whites until stiff peaks form. Whisk one-third into egg yolk mixture; fold in remaining whites. Pour into greased 8-inch (2 L) square glass baking dish.

Bake tomatoes and soufflé in centre of 400°F (200°C) oven until tomatoes are shrivelled, about 25 minutes, and soufflé is puffed, dark golden and top is firm to the touch, about 30 minutes. Sprinkle tomatoes with basil; serve with soufflé.

PER SERVING: about 400 cal, 22 g pro, 28 g total fat (11 g sat. fat), 14 g carb, 2 g fibre, 408 mg chol, 939 mg sodium. % RDI: 16% calcium, 16% iron, 33% vit A, 33% vit C, 31% folate.

EGGS & CHEESE

Spinach & Rapini Curry with Paneer

Prep: 10 minutes   **Cook:** 40 minutes   **Makes:** 8 servings

⅓ cup (75 mL) **vegetable oil**
3 cloves **garlic,** minced
1 tbsp (15 mL) **cumin seeds**
1½ tsp (7 mL) **paprika**
¾ tsp (4 mL) **salt**
½ tsp (2 mL) **turmeric**
½ tsp (2 mL) **cayenne pepper**
1 bottle (680 mL) **strained tomatoes** (passata)

Homemade Paneer (page 260) or 1 lb (500 g) paneer, cut into 1-inch (2.5 cm) cubes
¾ cup (175 mL) **whipping cream**
16 cups (4 L) lightly packed **fresh spinach leaves,** chopped
1 bunch **rapini** (leaves only), chopped

In Dutch oven, heat 2 tbsp (30 mL) of the oil over medium heat; fry garlic and cumin seeds, stirring, until seeds begin to pop and garlic is golden, about 2 minutes.

Stir in paprika, salt, turmeric and cayenne; cook, stirring, for 1 minute.

Stir in strained tomatoes and 2 cups (500 mL) water; bring to boil. Reduce heat and simmer, covered, for 30 minutes.

Meanwhile, in nonstick skillet, heat remaining oil over medium-high heat; fry paneer, in batches and turning often, until golden all over, about 5 minutes. Transfer to paper towel–lined plate.

Return sauce to boil; stir in cream. Add spinach and rapini; reduce heat and simmer until wilted, about 5 minutes. Stir in paneer; cook until heated through, about 2 minutes.

PER SERVING: about 380 cal, 16 g pro, 29 g total fat (13 g sat. fat), 19 g carb, 5 g fibre, 75 mg chol, 427 mg sodium. % RDI: 45% calcium, 40% iron, 96% vit A, 50% vit C, 65% folate.

Rustic Spinach & Feta Galette

Prep: 30 minutes **Stand:** 30 minutes **Cook:** 55 minutes **Makes:** 8 servings

1¾ cups (425 mL) **all-purpose flour**

1 tsp (5 mL) **baking powder**

½ tsp (2 mL) **salt**

⅓ cup (75 mL) **extra-virgin olive oil**

⅓ cup (75 mL) **milk**

1 **egg**

FILLING:

2 tbsp (30 mL) **extra-virgin olive oil**

1 **sweet onion,** diced

5 **green onions,** thinly sliced

3 bags (each 10 oz/284 g) **fresh spinach,** trimmed

1½ cups (375 mL) crumbled **feta cheese**

¾ cup (175 mL) shredded **mozzarella cheese**

2 **eggs**

½ cup (125 mL) chopped **fresh mint**

½ cup (125 mL) chopped **fresh dill**

½ cup (125 mL) chopped **fresh parsley**

½ tsp (2 mL) each **salt** and **pepper**

Pinch **ground cloves**

1 **egg,** beaten

1 tsp (5 mL) **sesame seeds**

*This free-form pie has classic Greek flavours and a distinctly olive oil–flavoured crust. Serve it warm or at room temperature.

Whisk flour, baking powder and salt. Whisk oil, milk and egg; pour over flour. Stir to form fairly smooth dough. On floured surface, knead until smooth, 2 minutes. Press into disc; wrap and refrigerate for 30 minutes.

FILLING: In skillet, heat oil over medium heat; fry sweet and green onions, stirring, until softened, 2 minutes. Transfer to large bowl. Rinse spinach; shake off excess water. In large pot, in batches, cook spinach, covered, over medium-high heat, stirring once, until wilted, 3 minutes. Drain; squeeze out moisture. Mix into onions along with feta, mozzarella, eggs, mint, dill, parsley, salt, pepper and cloves.

On floured surface, roll out dough to 16-inch (40 cm) circle. Fit into greased 9-inch (23 cm) cast-iron skillet, letting excess hang over edge. Mound filling in centre; lift pastry up over filling, letting fall naturally into folds and leaving 5-inch (12 cm) opening in centre. Brush dough with beaten egg; sprinkle with sesame seeds. Bake in bottom third of 375°F (190°C) oven until pastry is golden and filling is steaming, about 45 minutes. Let stand for 10 minutes before cutting into wedges.

PER SERVING: about 407 cal, 17 g pro, 25 g total fat (9 g sat. fat), 31 g carb, 4 g fibre, 129 mg chol, 838 mg sodium, 685 mg potassium. % RDI: 39% calcium, 46% iron, 122% vit A, 30% vit C, 112% folate.

Whole Wheat Chive Crêpes with Spinach & Gruyère

Prep: 35 minutes   **Stand:** 1 hour   **Cook:** 1½ hours   **Makes:** 6 servings

⅔ cup (150 mL) **whole wheat flour**

⅔ cup (150 mL) **all-purpose flour**

¼ tsp (1 mL) **salt**

4 eggs

1½ cups (375 mL) **milk**

¼ cup (60 mL) **butter,** melted

1 tbsp (15 mL) chopped **fresh chives**

1 tbsp (15 mL) chopped **fresh parsley**

BÉCHAMEL SAUCE:

2 tbsp (30 mL) **butter**

¼ cup (60 mL) **all-purpose flour**

2 cups (500 mL) **milk**

¼ tsp (1 mL) each **salt** and **pepper**

Pinch **nutmeg**

1 cup (250 mL) grated **Parmesan cheese**

FILLING:

2 tbsp (30 mL) **extra-virgin olive oil**

3 **shallots** or half small onion, finely chopped

1 pkg (1 lb/500 g) **fresh spinach,** trimmed

¼ tsp (1 mL) each **salt** and **pepper**

2 cups (500 mL) shredded **Gruyère** or Swiss **cheese**

Whisk together whole wheat flour, all-purpose flour and salt. Whisk together eggs, milk and 2 tbsp (30 mL) of the butter; pour over dry ingredients and whisk until smooth. Strain through sieve into clean bowl. Stir in chives. Refrigerate, covered, for 1 hour.

Heat 8-inch (20 cm) crêpe pan or skillet over medium heat. For each crêpe, brush with some of the remaining butter. Pour scant ¼ cup (60 mL) batter into centre of pan, swirling pan to coat; cook, turning once, until golden, about 1 minute. Transfer to plate. (To store, layer between waxed paper and wrap in plastic wrap; refrigerate for up to 24 hours or freeze in airtight container for up to 1 month.)

BÉCHAMEL SAUCE: In saucepan, melt butter over medium heat; whisk in flour. Cook, whisking, for 2 minutes.

Whisk in milk, salt, pepper and nutmeg; bring to boil. Reduce heat and simmer, whisking often, until smooth and thickened, about 10 minutes. Reserve 2 tbsp (30 mL) of the Parmesan cheese; whisk in remaining cheese. Keep warm.

FILLING: In large saucepan, heat oil over medium heat; fry shallots until golden and softened, about 3 minutes.

In batches, add spinach to pan; cook, stirring, until wilted and no liquid remains, about 8 minutes. Transfer to sieve; squeeze out liquid. Coarsely chop spinach; sprinkle with salt and pepper.

Spread 2 tbsp (30 mL) of the Béchamel Sauce on each crêpe. Divide spinach mixture over top. Sprinkle each with heaping 2 tbsp (30 mL) Gruyère cheese. Roll up snugly. Arrange in single layer, seam side down, in 13- x 9-inch (3 L) glass baking dish.

Spread with remaining béchamel; sprinkle with reserved Parmesan cheese. Bake in 350°F (180°C) oven until cheese is melted, 40 to 45 minutes. Sprinkle with parsley.

PER SERVING: about 623 cal, 33 g pro, 40 g total fat (21 g sat. fat), 35 g carb, 4 g fibre, 222 mg chol, 898 mg sodium. % RDI: 78% calcium, 33% iron, 106% vit A, 13% vit C, 77% folate.

[VEGETABLES

Spaghetti Squash
with Roasted Tomatoes
(page 222)

Roasted Red Pepper & Sweet
Potato Soup (opposite) with
Three-Seed Biscuits (page 261)

Roasted Red Pepper & Sweet Potato Soup

Prep: 20 minutes   **Cook:** 1¼ hours   **Makes:** 4 servings

3 **sweet red peppers,** chopped

2 **sweet potatoes,** peeled and cubed (about 1 lb/500 g)

1 **onion,** chopped

3 cloves **garlic**

2 tbsp (30 mL) **olive oil**

1 tsp (5 mL) **dried Italian herb seasoning** or dried basil

¼ tsp (1 mL) each **salt** and **pepper**

4 cups (1 L) **vegetable broth**

½ cup (125 mL) **Balkan-style plain yogurt**

2 tbsp (30 mL) chopped **fresh parsley**

In roasting pan, toss together red peppers, sweet potatoes, onion, garlic, oil, Italian seasoning, salt and pepper. Roast in 425°F (220°C) oven, stirring once, until tender, about 1 hour.

In food processor, in batches, purée vegetables with broth; strain into saucepan. Whisk in 1 cup (250 mL) water. Bring soup to boil; reduce heat and simmer for 5 minutes.

Meanwhile, stir yogurt with parsley. Dollop on bowls of soup.

VEGETABLES

PER SERVING: about 242 cal, 5 g pro, 10 g total fat (3 g sat. fat), 38 g carb, 3 g fibre, 11 mg chol, 1,218 mg sodium. % RDI: 10% calcium, 13% iron, 249% vit A, 278% vit C, 14% folate.

Thai Cold Salad Rolls

Prep: 30 minutes   **Stand:** 10 minutes   **Makes:** 24 pieces

4 oz (125 g) **rice stick vermicelli**

Half **English cucumber,** peeled, halved and cored

1 **sweet red pepper,** halved and seeded

1 large **carrot,** peeled

1 **mango,** peeled and pitted

12 **rice paper wrappers** (about 6 inches/15 cm)

12 large **fresh mint** or basil **leaves**

¼ cup (60 mL) finely chopped **roasted peanuts**

DIPPING SAUCE:

½ cup (125 mL) **sweet Thai chili sauce**

2 tbsp (30 mL) **lime juice**

2 tsp (10 mL) **unseasoned rice vinegar**

DIPPING SAUCE: Stir together chili sauce, lime juice, vinegar and 2 tsp (10 mL) water.

Soak rice vermicelli in hot water until tender, about 10 minutes. Drain. Toss with 1 tbsp (15 mL) of the Dipping Sauce.

Cut cucumber, red pepper, carrot and mango into 3- x ⅛-inch (8 cm x 3 mm) strips.

Fill shallow pan with lukewarm water. Soak rice paper wrappers, 1 at a time, in water until soft and pliable, about 1 minute. Transfer to tea towel; pat dry.

Along bottom edge of wrapper and leaving 1 inch (2.5 cm) uncovered on each side, place 1 mint leaf, 1 tsp (5 mL) of the peanuts, 4 pieces each of the cucumber, red pepper, carrot and mango, and about 1 tbsp (15 mL) of the vermicelli. Fold sides in and tightly roll up. Repeat with remaining ingredients to make 12 rolls. (To store, place, seam side down, on plastic wrap–lined plate or baking sheet. Cover with damp towel and overwrap in plastic wrap; refrigerate for up to 8 hours.)

Cut crosswise in half. Serve with remaining Dipping Sauce.

PER PIECE WITH 1 TSP (5 ML) SAUCE: about 54 cal, 1 g pro, 1 g total fat (trace sat. fat), 10 g carb, 1 g fibre, 0 mg chol, 53 mg sodium, 58 mg potassium. % RDI: 1% calcium, 1% iron, 10% vit A, 20% vit C, 3% folate.

Potato Mushroom Goulash

Prep: 12 minutes   **Stand:** 15 minutes   **Cook:** 40 minutes
Makes: 8 to 10 servings

✳ Homemade Roasted Vegetable Stock is best for this creamy Eastern European soup. For a lighter-flavoured version, replace with 3 cups (750 mL) store-bought vegetable broth combined with 2 cups (500 mL) water.

1 pkg (½ oz/14 g) **dried oyster mushrooms**

¾ cup (175 mL) **hot water**

3 tbsp (45 mL) **butter**

2½ cups (625 mL) diced **onions**

1½ cups (375 mL) diced **leeks** (white and light green parts only)

1 lb (500 g) **white mushrooms,** quartered

5 cups (1.25 L) diced peeled **potatoes**

4 cups (1 L) **Roasted Vegetable Stock** (page 255)

½ tsp (2 mL) **salt**

¼ tsp (1 mL) **caraway seeds**

¼ tsp (1 mL) **sweet Hungarian paprika**

¾ cup (175 mL) **sour cream**

Soak dried mushrooms in hot water until softened, about 15 minutes. Reserving soaking liquid, strain mushrooms through fine-mesh sieve; mince.

In Dutch oven or large saucepan, heat butter over medium-low heat; fry onions, leeks, and soaked and white mushrooms until softened, about 10 minutes.

Add potatoes; cook, stirring, for 5 minutes. Add stock, reserved soaking liquid, salt, caraway seeds and paprika; bring to boil. Reduce heat and simmer, covered, until potatoes are tender enough to fall apart, about 20 minutes. Stir in sour cream.

PER EACH OF 10 SERVINGS: about 177 cal, 4 g pro, 7 g total fat (4 g sat. fat), 27 g carb, 3 g fibre, 16 mg chol, 270 mg sodium, 521 mg potassium. % RDI: 5% calcium, 11% iron, 51% vit A, 22% vit C, 18% folate.

Vegetarian Ceviche

Prep: 10 minutes   **Stand:** 10 minutes   **Makes:** twenty ¼-cup (60 mL) servings

2 tbsp (30 mL) **lime juice**

¼ tsp (1 mL) each **salt** and **pepper**

⅓ cup (75 mL) **olive oil** or avocado oil

3 tbsp (45 mL) chopped **fresh coriander** or parsley

Half **jalapeño pepper,** seeded and minced

1 can (14 oz/398 mL) **hearts of palm,** drained and rinsed

2 **avocados,** peeled and pitted

2 cups (500 mL) **grape** or cherry **tomatoes,** quartered

½ cup (125 mL) finely diced **red onion,** rinsed and drained

½ cup (125 mL) chopped **green olives**

In large bowl, whisk together lime juice, salt and pepper. Whisk in oil until thickened. Stir in coriander and jalapeño.

Cut hearts of palm into thin rings and avocados into ½-inch (1 cm) pieces; add to bowl along with tomatoes, onion and olives. Toss to coat. Let stand for 10 minutes or, refrigerated, up to 6 hours.

✳ Commonly served throughout Central and South America, *ceviche* is, by definition, a raw seafood salad "cooked" by citrus juice. This vegetarian version is designed to be mounded on or scooped up with crispy tostadas or tortilla chips.

VEGETABLES

PER SERVING: about 77 cal, 1 g pro, 7 g total fat (1 g sat. fat), 4 g carb, 2 g fibre, 0 mg chol, 137 mg sodium, 165 mg potassium. % RDI: 1% calcium, 4% iron, 2% vit A, 10% vit C, 11% folate.

Corn Tempura

Prep: 15 minutes **Cook:** 8 minutes **Makes:** 6 servings

1 cup (250 mL) **ice water**
¾ cup (175 mL) **all-purpose flour**
¼ cup (60 mL) **cornstarch**
½ tsp (1 mL) **baking soda**
1 **egg**
2 cups (500 mL) **fresh corn kernels**
Vegetable oil for deep-frying

DIPPING SAUCE:

¼ cup (60 mL) **tempura dipping sauce** (such as Kikkoman)
¼ cup (60 mL) grated **daikon radish**

In bowl, whisk together ½ cup (125 mL) of the ice water, flour, cornstarch, baking soda and egg. Whisk in remaining ice water, ¼ cup (60 mL) at a time, to make thin batter. Stir in corn. Place bowl in second bowl filled with more ice water.

Pour enough oil into wok or Dutch oven to come about 2 inches (5 cm) up side; heat until 375°F (190°C) on deep-fry thermometer, or until 1-inch (2.5 cm) cube of white bread turns golden in 30 seconds.

Gently drop batter, 2 tbsp (30 mL) at a time, into hot oil (batter will sink slightly then rise to surface with bits breaking off at edges). Deep-fry, turning once, until golden, about 3 minutes. Drain on paper towel–lined rack.

DIPPING SAUCE: In small saucepan, bring dipping sauce and ¼ cup (60 mL) water to boil; remove from heat. Squeeze out liquid from radish; add radish to sauce. Serve with tempura.

✳ This batter is very thin, much like crêpe batter. Keeping it cold in an ice bath is important because it helps make the tempura crispy and light. Both tempura dipping sauce and daikon radish are available in some supermarkets and in Asian grocery stores.

VEGETABLES

217

PER SERVING: about 299 cal, 4 g pro, 18 g total fat (2 g sat. fat), 31 g carb, 2 g fibre, 31 mg chol, 794 mg sodium, 143 mg potassium. % RDI: 1% calcium, 8% iron, 2% vit A, 5% vit C, 25% folate.

Sautéed Greens with Garlic

Prep: 5 minutes   **Cook:** 5 minutes   **Makes:** 4 servings

* When in season, find greens at local farmer's markets. No matter which type you choose, blanched and sautéed greens make a lovely side dish. Pick your greens and use the chart opposite for amounts and cooking times.

2 tbsp (30 mL) **olive oil**
2 cloves **garlic,** minced
¼ tsp (1 mL) **hot pepper flakes**

Blanched Greens (opposite)
Pinch **salt**
Half **lemon**

In skillet, heat oil over medium-high heat; sauté garlic and hot pepper flakes until garlic is golden, about 20 seconds. Add greens; sprinkle with salt. Cook, tossing to coat, until heated through, 3 to 5 minutes.

Squeeze lemon juice over greens just before serving.

PER SERVING: about 76 cal, 2 g pro, 7 g total fat (1 g sat. fat), 3 g carb, 1 g fibre, 0 mg chol, 307 mg sodium. % RDI: 10% calcium, 9% iron, 49% vit A, 50% vit C, 21% folate.

VEGETABLES

BLANCHED GREENS

✳ Leafy greens can be quite gritty. To clean them, plunge into plenty of cold water. Swirl around to loosen and remove any grit; let stand for 1 minute. Lift greens out of water and drain. Repeat two or three times, depending on amount of sand and grit. Then use a salad spinner to dry them. (Hint: This same method also works well with sliced leeks; bunches of delicate fresh herbs, such as coriander, parsley and basil; and, of course, salad greens.)

• Young greens are generally more tender and cook faster than mature greens. These are just guidelines to leave a bit of crunch.

• Prepare as directed in chart. Cook, covered, in large pot of boiling salted water for recommended time. Drain and chill under cold water; drain again. Squeeze out liquid. Pat dry.

GREENS	PREPARATION	COOKING TIME
1 lb (500 g) **baby bok choy** (about 10 heads)	Halve lengthwise	3 to 6 minutes
1 lb (500 g) **kale** (about 1 bunch)	Discard tough stems and ribs; coarsely chop leaves	3 to 5 minutes
1½ lb (750 g) **Swiss chard** (about 1½ bunches)	Discard bottom 1 inch (2.5 cm) of stems; coarsely chop remaining stems and leaves	2 to 4 minutes
2 lb (1 kg) **collard greens** (about 2 bunches)	Discard tough stems and ribs; coarsely chop leaves	8 to 12 minutes
1 lb (500 g) **rapini** (about 1 bunch)	Discard bottom ¼ inch (5 mm) of stalks	4 to 5 minutes
1 lb (500 g) **Broccolini** (about 2 bunches)	Discard bottom ¼ inch (5 mm) of stalks	4 to 5 minutes

Cider-Glazed Roasted Vegetables

Prep: 20 minutes   **Cook:** 1¼ hours   **Makes:** 8 to 10 servings

*For a main course, serve with couscous, quinoa or rice. If you have a large enough roasting pan, you can cook all the vegetables in one pan, adding the second batch of veggies as directed.

1 **rutabaga** (2 lb/1 kg), peeled and cut into ¾-inch (2 cm) cubes

4 **parsnips** (1 lb/500 g), peeled and cut into 1-inch (2.5 cm) cubes

1 cup (250 mL) **apple cider**

¼ cup (60 mL) **butter,** melted

4 tsp (20 mL) minced **fresh thyme**

1 tsp (5 mL) **salt**

½ tsp (2 mL) **pepper**

3 **leeks** (white and light green parts only), cut into 1-inch (2.5 cm) thick rounds

2 **sweet red peppers,** cut into 2-inch (5 cm) pieces

1 large bulb **fennel,** trimmed and cut into 2-inch (5 cm) pieces

1 head **garlic,** separated into cloves and peeled

Toss together rutabaga, parsnips and half each of the cider, butter, thyme, salt and pepper. Spread in greased 13- x 9-inch (3 L) glass baking dish or small roasting pan. Cover with foil; roast in 425°F (220°C) oven for 15 minutes.

Meanwhile, toss together leeks, red peppers, fennel, garlic and remaining cider, butter, thyme, salt and pepper. Spread in separate same-size greased baking dish or roasting pan; cover with foil. Add to oven; roast for 30 minutes.

Uncover both pans; stir vegetables. Roast, stirring occasionally, until tender, golden and almost no juices remain, about 30 minutes.

PER EACH OF 10 SERVINGS: about 142 cal, 3 g pro, 5 g total fat (3 g sat. fat), 24 g carb, 4 g fibre, 12 mg chol, 301 mg sodium. % RDI: 8% calcium, 11% iron, 17% vit A, 107% vit C, 24% folate.

VEGETABLES

Spaghetti Squash with Roasted Tomatoes

Prep: 15 minutes   **Cook:** 1 hour   **Makes:** 6 servings

* Stir ¼ cup (60 mL) grated Parmesan cheese or nutritional yeast into the cooked and shredded squash if desired. Both offer lovely cheesy, nutty flavour.

1 **spaghetti squash** (2½ lb/1.25 kg)
½ tsp (2 mL) each **salt** and **pepper**
4 cups (1 L) **grape** or cherry **tomatoes,** halved
3 cloves **garlic,** minced
2 tbsp (30 mL) **olive oil**

1 tbsp (15 mL) **red wine vinegar**
¼ tsp (1 mL) **hot pepper flakes**
1 can (19 oz/540 mL) **white kidney beans** or navy beans, drained and rinsed
3 tbsp (45 mL) chopped **fresh parsley**

Halve and seed squash. Bake, cut side down, on greased baking sheet in 400°F (200°C) oven until flesh is tender when pierced, about 1 hour. Using fork, scrape strands into bowl; stir in half each of the salt and pepper. Keep warm.

Meanwhile, in 13- x 9-inch (3 L) glass baking dish, toss together tomatoes, garlic, oil, vinegar, hot pepper flakes and remaining salt and pepper. Roast in 400°F (200°C) oven for 30 minutes. Stir in beans and parsley; roast until beans are heated through and tomatoes are shrivelled, about 10 minutes. Mound squash on platter; spoon tomato mixture over top.

VEGETABLES

PER SERVING: about 166 cal, 6 g pro, 6 g total fat (1 g sat. fat), 26 g carb, 8 g fibre, 0 mg chol, 428 mg sodium, 588 mg potassium. % RDI: 6% calcium, 13% iron, 11% vit A, 33% vit C, 22% folate.

Dilled Potato & Grilled Corn Salad

Prep: 12 minutes   **Stand:** 10 minutes   **Cook:** 30 minutes
Makes: 6 to 8 servings

4 **cobs of corn,** husked

3 tbsp (45 mL) **vegetable oil**

2 lb (1 kg) small **red** or white **potatoes** (about 30), peeled

4 **green onions,** sliced

2 tsp (10 mL) **grainy mustard**

½ tsp (2 mL) **salt**

¼ tsp (1 mL) **pepper**

¼ cup (60 mL) **wine vinegar**

2 tbsp (30 mL) chopped **fresh dill**

Brush corn with 1 tbsp (15 mL) of the oil. Grill, covered, on greased grill over medium-high heat until tender and slightly charred, 10 to 15 minutes. Let cool. Cut off kernels; place in large bowl.

In large saucepan of boiling salted water, cook potatoes, covered, until tender, about 15 minutes. Drain and halve; add to bowl along with onions, mustard, salt and pepper. Sprinkle with vinegar; toss well. Let cool.

Add remaining oil and dill; toss to coat.

VEGETABLES

PER EACH OF 8 SERVINGS: about 197 cal, 4 g pro, 6 g total fat (1 g sat. fat), 34 g carb, 4 g fibre, 0 mg chol, 400 mg sodium, 641 mg potassium. % RDI: 2% calcium, 10% iron, 2% vit A, 37% vit C, 22% folate.

Dilled Potato & Grilled Corn Salad
(page 223)

Swiss Chard Double-Crust Pizza

Prep: 30 minutes **Stand:** 2¼ hours **Cook:** 1¼ hours **Makes:** 8 servings

3 tbsp (45 mL) **olive oil**

1 **onion,** chopped

1 clove **garlic,** minced

2 bunches **Swiss chard** (about 2 lb/1 kg total), trimmed, stems thinly sliced and leaves coarsely chopped

½ tsp (2 mL) **salt**

Pinch **hot pepper flakes**

1 **egg yolk** or 2 tbsp (30 mL) milk

DOUGH:

1 tsp (5 mL) **granulated sugar**

1½ cups (375 mL) **warm water**

1 pkg **active dry yeast** (or 2¼ tsp/11 mL)

1 tbsp (15 mL) **olive oil**

3½ cups (875 mL) **all-purpose flour**

½ tsp (2 mL) **salt**

DOUGH: Dissolve sugar in warm water. Sprinkle in yeast; let stand until frothy, 10 minutes. Stir in oil. In large bowl, mix 3 cups (750 mL) of the flour with salt; make well in centre. Pour yeast mixture into well; stir flour into liquid a bit at a time. Turn out onto floured surface. Knead, adding remaining flour as necessary, until smooth and elastic, 8 minutes.

Place in greased bowl, turning to grease all over. Let rise, covered, in warm place until doubled in bulk, about 2 hours. (Or, refrigerate for 12 to 24 hours; let stand at room temperature for 1 hour before rolling.)

Meanwhile, in large skillet, heat oil over medium-high heat; sauté onion and garlic until softened, 2 minutes. Add Swiss chard, salt and hot pepper flakes; cook until mixture is dry, 15 to 20 minutes. Let cool.

Punch down dough; divide in half. On lightly floured surface, stretch or roll out half to 16- x 11-inch (40 x 28 cm) rectangle. Place on greased 15- x 10-inch (38 x 25 cm) rimmed baking sheet. Spread Swiss chard mixture over dough, leaving 1-inch (2.5 cm) border at edges. Stretch or roll out remaining dough to 15- x 10-inch (38 x 25 cm) rectangle; place over Swiss chard. Pull up overhang; pinch edges together. Flute if desired. Whisk egg yolk with 2 tsp (10 mL) water; brush over top.

Bake in bottom third of 375°F (190°C) oven until bottom is golden, 45 to 55 minutes. Let stand for 10 minutes before cutting.

PER SERVING: about 305 cal, 9 g pro, 10 g total fat (2 g sat. fat), 50 g carb, 5 g fibre, 25 mg chol, 545 mg sodium, 880 mg potassium. % RDI: 10% calcium, 45% iron, 45% vit A, 40% vit C, 70% folate.

Triple Mushroom Tart

Prep: 30 minutes   **Stand:** 1 hour   **Cook:** 1¼ hours   **Makes:** 8 servings

1 pkg (½ oz/14 g) **dried porcini mushrooms**

½ cup (125 mL) **dry white wine**

2 tbsp (30 mL) **butter**

1 **leek** (white and light green parts only), thinly sliced

3 cloves **garlic,** minced

3 cups (750 mL) sliced **white** or cremini **mushrooms** (about 10 oz/300 g)

2 cups (500 mL) sliced **oyster mushrooms** (about 6 oz/175 g)

¾ tsp (4 mL) **salt**

½ tsp (2 mL) **pepper**

2 tsp (10 mL) chopped **fresh thyme**

1 cup (250 mL) **whipping cream**

PASTRY:

1 cup (250 mL) **all-purpose flour**

½ tsp (2 mL) **baking powder**

¼ tsp (1 mL) **salt**

½ cup (125 mL) cold **unsalted butter,** cubed

¼ cup (60 mL) **sour cream**

1 **egg yolk**

PASTRY: Combine flour, baking powder and salt. With pastry blender or 2 knives, cut in butter until in pea-size pieces. Whisk sour cream with egg yolk; stir in flour mixture just until dough comes together. Press into disc; wrap and refrigerate for 30 minutes.

Microwave porcini with wine at high until hot, 1 minute. In skillet, melt butter over medium heat; fry leek and garlic until softened, 3 minutes. Increase heat to medium-high; add white and oyster mushrooms, salt and pepper. Sauté until no liquid remains, 8 to 10 minutes.

Meanwhile, reserving soaking liquid, strain porcinis; coarsely chop. Add porcinis and liquid to skillet; stir in thyme. Cook, stirring, until almost no liquid remains, 1 minute. Stir in cream; cook until sauce is golden and thickly coats mushrooms, 8 minutes. Let cool.

On floured surface, roll out dough to 11-inch (28 cm) circle. Press over bottom and up side of 9-inch (23 cm) tart pan with removable bottom; tuck in overhang to make level with rim. Prick bottom all over with fork; refrigerate for 30 minutes. Spread filling in shell. Bake in centre of 350°F (180°C) oven until golden and set, 45 minutes. Let stand for 10 minutes.

PER SERVING: about 330 cal, 5 g pro, 27 g total fat (17 g sat. fat), 19 g carb, 2 g fibre, 105 mg chol, 350 mg sodium, 277 mg potassium. % RDI: 5% calcium, 14% iron, 24% vit A, 3% vit C, 23% folate.

* Heady with fragrant mushrooms, just a small wedge of this rich and decadent tart is enough. Serve with a simple peppery arugula or other leafy green salad.

VEGETABLES

Roasted Cherry Tomato Tart

Prep: 15 minutes **Stand:** 1 hour **Cook:** 45 minutes **Makes:** 6 to 8 servings

4 cups (1 L) **grape** or **cherry tomatoes**

4 tsp (20 mL) **extra-virgin olive oil**

1 clove **garlic,** minced

¼ tsp (1 mL) each **salt** and **pepper**

1 tbsp (15 mL) **Dijon mustard**

½ cup (125 mL) crumbled **goat cheese**

8 **Kalamata olives,** quartered

PASTRY:

1 cup (250 mL) **all-purpose flour**

½ cup (125 mL) **cornmeal**

2 tsp (10 mL) chopped **fresh thyme**

½ tsp (2 mL) **salt**

½ cup (125 mL) cold **unsalted butter,** diced

3 tbsp (45 mL) **ice water**

2 tsp (10 mL) **lemon juice** or vinegar

＊ To make tartlets instead of one big tart, divide dough into sixths; roll out each to 5½-inch (13 cm) round. Fit into 4-inch (10 cm) tart pans with removable bottoms. Reduce baking times for shells and filled tarts by 2 minutes each.

PASTRY: In food processor, blend together flour, cornmeal, thyme and salt; pulse in butter until in fine crumbs with a few larger pieces. With motor running, add ice water and lemon juice all at once; pulse just until dough starts to clump together. Remove and press into disc. Wrap and refrigerate until chilled, about 30 minutes. (Or, refrigerate for up to 2 days; let come to room temperature before continuing.)

On floured surface, roll out dough to 11-inch (28 cm) circle. Press into bottom and up side of 9-inch (23 cm) tart pan with removable bottom, folding in edge and tucking overhang behind pastry to make level with rim. Prick all over with fork. Refrigerate for 30 minutes or up to 24 hours. Bake in bottom third of 400°F (200°C) oven until golden, 18 to 20 minutes. Let cool on rack.

Meanwhile, in 13- x 9-inch (3 L) glass baking dish, toss together tomatoes, oil, garlic, salt and pepper. Roast in 400°F (200°C) oven until slightly charred and shrivelled, about 30 minutes.

Brush bottom of baked tart shell with mustard; sprinkle with all but 2 tbsp (30 mL) of the goat cheese. Arrange tomato mixture over top; dot with olives and sprinkle with remaining goat cheese.

Bake in centre of 400°F (200°C) oven until filling is hot, about 14 minutes. Serve warm or at room temperature.

PER EACH OF 8 SERVINGS: about 260 cal, 5 g pro, 17 g total fat (9 g sat. fat), 22 g carb, 2 g fibre, 35 mg chol, 440 mg sodium. % RDI: 3% calcium, 10% iron, 19% vit A, 17% vit C, 26% folate.

VEGETABLES

Meatless Polpette in Tomato Sauce

Prep: 15 minutes **Stand:** 30 minutes **Cook:** 50 minutes
Makes: 4 to 5 servings

✳ *Polpette,* or Italian meatballs, are fantastic with a side of sautéed rapini or other leafy green (see Sautéed Greens with Garlic, page 218). Or serve with cooked pasta, quinoa or rice.

2 cups (500 mL) **dry bread crumbs**
½ cup (125 mL) grated **Parmesan cheese**
1 tsp (5 mL) **baking powder**
¼ tsp (1 mL) **salt**
2 **eggs**
1 cup (250 mL) **milk**
¼ cup (60 mL) chopped **fresh parsley**
¼ cup (60 mL) **olive oil**

TOMATO SAUCE:

1 tbsp (15 mL) **olive oil**
1 **onion,** diced
1 clove **garlic,** minced
1 can (28 oz/796 mL) **crushed tomatoes**
1 can (5½ oz/156 mL) **tomato paste**
½ cup (125 mL) **dry white wine**
1 tsp (5 mL) **salt**
2 tbsp (30 mL) **fresh basil leaves,** sliced

Mix together bread crumbs, Parmesan cheese, baking powder and salt; stir in eggs, milk and parsley. With oiled hands, shape into 20 balls; place on tray. Refrigerate for 30 minutes.

TOMATO SAUCE: In large saucepan, heat oil over medium heat; fry onion and garlic until onion is softened, about 3 minutes. Add 1½ cups (375 mL) water, tomatoes, tomato paste, wine and salt; simmer until thickened, about 25 minutes.

Meanwhile, in large skillet, heat oil over medium-high heat; fry balls, turning often, until golden all over, about 4 minutes. Using slotted spoon, transfer to sauce. Cover and simmer until firm inside, about 20 minutes. Stir in basil.

PER EACH OF 5 SERVINGS: about 459 cal, 18 g pro, 20 g total fat (5 g sat. fat), 56 g carb, 7 g fibre, 87 mg chol, 1,405 mg sodium, 1,125 mg potassium. % RDI: 34% calcium, 44% iron, 25% vit A, 43% vit C, 38% folate.

Oven-Roasted Ratatouille on Cornmeal Pancakes

Prep: 20 minutes   **Stand:** 30 minutes   **Cook:** 45 minutes   **Makes:** 6 servings

1 **eggplant** (about 1 lb/500 g)

2 **zucchini** (about 1 lb/500 g)

1½ tsp (7 mL) **salt**

3 tbsp (45 mL) **olive oil**

2 tbsp (30 mL) chopped **fresh thyme**

¼ tsp (1 mL) **pepper**

1 each **sweet red** and **green pepper**

6 cups (1.5 L) **grape** or cherry **tomatoes,** halved

1 large **onion,** diced

12 small cloves **garlic,** peeled

⅓ cup (75 mL) halved **Kalamata olives**

1 tbsp (15 mL) **red wine vinegar**

CORNMEAL PANCAKES:

⅔ cup (150 mL) **all-purpose flour**

⅓ cup (75 mL) **cornmeal**

1 tsp (5 mL) **baking powder**

½ tsp (2 mL) **baking soda**

½ tsp (2 mL) **granulated sugar**

¼ tsp (1 mL) each **salt** and **pepper**

2 **eggs**

1 cup (250 mL) **buttermilk**

3 tbsp (45 mL) **olive oil**

¼ cup (60 mL) thinly sliced **green onions** or chives

Peel eggplant; cut eggplant and zucchini into ½-inch (1 cm) pieces. In colander in sink, toss with 1 tsp (5 mL) of the salt; weigh down with plate. Let drain for 30 minutes. Pat dry with paper towel.

Toss together eggplant, zucchini, and half each of the oil, thyme and pepper; spread on parchment paper–lined or greased large baking sheet. Cut red and green peppers into ½-inch (1 cm) pieces; toss together with tomatoes, onion, garlic, and remaining salt, oil, thyme and pepper. Spread on separate parchment paper–lined or greased large baking sheet.

Bake in top and bottom thirds of 400°F (200°C) oven, switching and rotating pans and stirring once, until softened and golden, about 45 minutes. Transfer to bowl; toss together with olives and vinegar. Keep warm.

CORNMEAL PANCAKES: Meanwhile, whisk together flour, cornmeal, baking powder, baking soda, sugar, salt and pepper. Whisk together eggs, buttermilk and 2 tbsp (30 mL) of the oil; pour over dry ingredients. Add onions; whisk just until combined.

Brush nonstick skillet with some of the remaining oil; heat over medium heat. In batches and using ¼ cup (60 mL) for each pancake, pour in batter. Cook until bottoms are golden and bubbles break on top, about 3 minutes. Turn; cook until bottoms are golden, 2 to 3 minutes. Serve topped with ratatouille.

PER SERVING: about 367 cal, 9 g pro, 20 g total fat (3 g sat. fat), 42 g carb, 7 g fibre, 65 mg chol, 951 mg sodium, 923 mg potassium. % RDI: 14% calcium, 19% iron, 34% vit A, 122% vit C, 47% folate.

Curried Potato Kale Galette

Prep: 15 minutes   **Cook:** 1 hour   **Makes:** 6 servings

✳ If you're using a springform pan that doesn't have the tightest of seals, place foil-lined roasting pan on rack underneath pan in oven to catch any drips. Or, wrap base of pan in foil.

2 tbsp (30 mL) **olive oil**

1 large **onion,** diced

3 cloves **garlic,** minced

1 tbsp (15 mL) minced **fresh ginger**

1 tsp (5 mL) **ground cumin**

1 tsp (5 mL) **garam masala**

1 tsp (5 mL) **salt**

½ tsp (2 mL) **turmeric**

Pinch **cayenne pepper**

8 cups (2 L) chopped **kale leaves** (about 1 bunch)

2 tsp (10 mL) lemon juice

4 **Yukon Gold potatoes** (about 2 lb/1 kg), peeled

3 tbsp (45 mL) **butter,** melted

In shallow Dutch oven or large saucepan, heat all but 1 tsp (5 mL) of the oil over medium heat; fry onion, garlic, ginger, cumin, garam masala, half of the salt, the turmeric and cayenne pepper, stirring often, until onion is softened, about 3 minutes.

Add kale and ¼ cup (60 mL) water; cook, covered, until wilted, about 4 minutes. Uncover and cook, scraping up any brown bits from bottom of pan, until no liquid remains, about 1 minute. Stir in lemon juice.

Brush bottom and side of 9-inch (2.5 L) springform pan or ovenproof skillet with remaining oil. Using mandoline or sharp knife, cut potatoes into paper-thin slices; toss with remaining salt. Spread one-third in pan; top with half of the kale mixture. Repeat layers once. Top with remaining potatoes, pressing to evenly distribute. Pour butter over top.

Bake, covered, in 425°F (220°C) oven until potatoes are tender when pierced with knife, about 50 minutes. Uncover and broil, watching closely, until golden on top, about 1 minute. Let stand for 10 minutes before cutting into wedges.

PER SERVING: about 253 cal, 5 g pro, 11 g total fat (4 g sat. fat), 36 g carb, 4 g fibre, 15 mg chol, 476 mg sodium. % RDI: 13% calcium, 17% iron, 128% vit A, 168% vit C, 16% folate.

Coconut Curried Eggplant

Prep: 10 minutes **Cook:** 30 minutes **Makes:** 4 servings

4 **Japanese eggplants**
   (about 1¼ lb/625 g total)

½ cup (125 mL) **vegetable oil**

1 **onion,** chopped

2 cloves **garlic,** minced

1 tbsp (15 mL) finely chopped **fresh coriander root**

¾ tsp (4 mL) **ground cumin**

¾ tsp (4 mL) **garam masala**

1 can (400 mL) **coconut milk**

1 **hot red pepper,** seeded and thinly sliced

1 **plum tomato,** chopped

½ tsp (2 mL) **salt**

2 tbsp (30 mL) chopped **fresh coriander leaves**

2 tsp (10 mL) **lemon juice**

＊ This quick and fabulous Thai-inspired main is best served with steamed jasmine rice.

Cut eggplants into 1-inch (2.5 cm) pieces. In large heavy skillet, heat oil over medium-high heat; in 2 batches, fry eggplant, turning once, until golden, about 8 minutes. Transfer to paper towel–lined plate to drain.

Drain off all but 2 tsp (10 mL) oil from pan; fry onion, garlic, coriander root, cumin and garam masala for 1 minute.

Add coconut milk, hot pepper, tomato and salt; bring to boil. Reduce heat and simmer until reduced by half, about 5 minutes. Stir in eggplant; cook until tender, about 5 minutes. Stir in chopped coriander and lemon juice.

VEGETABLES

PER SERVING: about 438 cal, 4 g pro, 41 g total fat (20 g sat. fat), 20 g carb, 5 g fibre, 0 mg chol, 305 mg sodium, 510 mg potassium. % RDI: 4% calcium, 29% iron, 3% vit A, 33% vit C, 18% folate.

Sweet Potato
& Cauliflower Tagine

Prep: 20 minutes   **Stand:** 5 minutes   **Cook:** 35 minutes   **Makes:** 4 servings

1 pkg (10 oz/284 g) **pearl onions**
   (2 cups/500 mL)

1 tbsp (15 mL) **vegetable oil**

3 cloves **garlic,** minced

1½ tsp (7 mL) **ground cumin**

1 tsp (5 mL) **paprika**

½ tsp (2 mL) **ground ginger**

½ tsp (2 mL) **salt**

¼ tsp (1 mL) **pepper**

¼ tsp (1 mL) **cayenne pepper**

3 cups (750 mL) cubed peeled
   sweet potato (1 large)

1 can (19 oz/540 mL) **chickpeas,**
   drained and rinsed

1½ cups (375 mL) **vegetable broth**

2 cups (500 mL) **cauliflower
   florets**

1 cup (250 mL) **frozen peas,**
   thawed

2 tbsp (25 mL) chopped **fresh
   coriander**

Place pearl onions in heatproof bowl; cover with boiling water.
Let stand for 5 minutes; drain and peel.

In shallow Dutch oven, heat oil over medium heat; fry pearl onions,
stirring occasionally, until golden, about 5 minutes. Add garlic, cumin,
paprika, ginger, salt, pepper and cayenne pepper; fry, stirring, for
1 minute.

Add sweet potato, chickpeas and broth; bring to boil. Reduce heat and
simmer, covered, for 5 minutes. Stir in cauliflower; simmer, covered,
until almost tender, about 20 minutes. Add peas; simmer, covered,
until hot. Sprinkle with coriander.

VEGETABLES

PER SERVING: about 337 cal, 11 g pro, 6 g total fat (1 g sat. fat), 63 g carb, 10 g fibre,
0 mg chol, 852 mg sodium. % RDI: 8% calcium, 24% iron, 177% vit A, 82% vit C,
55% folate.

Swiss Chard Dolmades with Tomato Sauce

Prep: 30 minutes   **Stand:** 10 minutes   **Cook:** 1½ hours   **Makes:** 8 servings

✳ The name *dolmades* comes from the Arabic word for "something stuffed." These fragrant rice-stuffed leaves are delectable. Choose Swiss chard with white stems, which usually mean thick leaves. Look for Puy lentils in specialty food stores. Serve with crusty bread to mop up all the saucy goodness.

⅓ cup (75 mL) **dried Puy** or green **lentils,** rinsed and drained

2 tbsp (30 mL) **extra-virgin olive oil**

1 **onion,** finely diced

1 cup (250 mL) **basmati rice**

2 tbsp (30 mL) **dried currants**

2 tbsp (30 mL) chopped **fresh dill**

½ tsp (2 mL) **dried mint**

¼ tsp (1 mL) each **salt** and **pepper**

Pinch **cinnamon**

Pinch **allspice**

½ cup (125 mL) crumbled **feta cheese**

2 tbsp (30 mL) toasted **pine nuts**

1 **egg,** beaten

1 bunch **Swiss chard** (about 1 lb/500 g)

TOMATO SAUCE:

2 tbsp (30 mL) **extra-virgin olive oil**

1 **onion,** diced

3 cloves **garlic,** minced

¼ tsp (1 mL) each **salt** and **pepper**

¼ tsp (1 mL) **ground allspice**

Pinch **granulated sugar**

Pinch **cayenne pepper**

1 can (28 oz/796 mL) **whole tomatoes**

TOMATO SAUCE: In saucepan, heat oil over medium-low heat; cook onion, stirring often, until golden, about 20 minutes.

Add garlic, salt, pepper, allspice, sugar and cayenne pepper; cook, stirring, for 3 minutes. Stir in tomatoes, breaking up with back of spoon; bring to boil. Reduce heat and simmer until slightly thickened, about 15 minutes. Purée in blender until smooth.

Meanwhile, in saucepan of boiling salted water, cook lentils until tender, about 20 minutes. Drain.

In separate saucepan, heat oil over medium-high heat; sauté onion until golden, about 5 minutes. Add rice, currants, dill, mint, salt, pepper, cinnamon and allspice; cook, stirring often, for 3 minutes.

Add 1¾ cups (425 mL) water; bring to boil. Reduce heat and simmer, covered, until no liquid remains, about 12 minutes. Turn off heat; let stand, covered, for 10 minutes. Stir in lentils, feta cheese, pine nuts and egg.

Trim ends from Swiss chard stems; trim off whole stem if thick and tough. In large pot of boiling salted water, blanch leaves for 1 minute. Drain and spread on clean towel; pat dry. Reserve 8 of the largest leaves; chop remaining leaves. Spread chopped leaves in lightly greased 13- x 9-inch (3 L) glass baking dish.

For each roll, place ½ cup (125 mL) rice mixture about 2 inches (5 cm) from stem end of reserved leaf; fold in sides and roll up. Arrange in baking dish.

Pour Tomato Sauce over rolls. Bake, covered, in 400°F (200°C) oven until steaming and bubbly, 25 to 30 minutes.

PER SERVING: about 266 cal, 8 g pro, 11 g total fat (3 g sat. fat), 35 g carb, 4 g fibre, 32 mg chol, 640 mg sodium. % RDI: 12% calcium, 25% iron, 18% vit A, 38% vit C, 30% folate.

Savoy Cabbage Gratin

Prep: 15 minutes **Cook:** 55 minutes **Makes:** 6 to 8 servings

1 head **savoy cabbage**
  (about 2 lb/1 kg)

2 tbsp (30 mL) **butter**

1 **leek** (white and light green parts
  only), thinly sliced

2 cloves **garlic,** minced

½ cup (125 mL) **vegetable broth**

½ tsp (2 mL) **salt**

¼ tsp (1 mL) **pepper**

¼ tsp (1 mL) **nutmeg**

2 tbsp (30 mL) **all-purpose flour**

1½ cups (375 mL) **10%** or **5% cream**

TOPPING:

¾ cup (175 mL) **fresh bread
  crumbs**

½ cup (125 mL) shredded **Gruyère
  cheese**

2 tbsp (30 mL) **butter,** melted

1 tsp (5 mL) chopped **fresh thyme,**
  chives or parsley

Quarter cabbage lengthwise; cut out and discard core. Thinly
slice cabbage.

In Dutch oven, melt butter over medium heat; fry leek and garlic,
stirring occasionally, until softened but not browned, about
10 minutes. Add cabbage, broth, salt, pepper and nutmeg; cook,
covered and stirring occasionally, until wilted, about 15 minutes.

Stir in flour; cook, stirring, for 2 minutes. Stir in cream; bring to boil.
Reduce heat and simmer until thickened, about 5 minutes. Spread in
greased 11- x 7-inch (2 L) baking dish.

TOPPING: Combine bread crumbs, Gruyère cheese, butter and thyme;
sprinkle over cabbage mixture.

Bake in 400°F (200°C) oven until bubbly and topping is golden, about
20 minutes.

PER EACH OF 8 SERVINGS: about 183 cal, 6 g pro, 13 g total fat (8 g sat. fat), 13 g
carb, 3 g fibre, 37 mg chol, 336 mg sodium. % RDI: 15% calcium, 6% iron, 20% vit A,
32% vit C, 28% folate.

Vegetable Curry with Squash

Prep: 18 minutes   **Cook:** 50 minutes   **Makes:** 4 to 6 servings

1½ cups (375 mL) cubed (1½ inch/ 4 cm) peeled **butternut squash**

1 cup (250 mL) cut (1 inch/2.5 cm) **green beans**

1 cup (250 mL) diced **carrots**

1 cup (250 mL) cubed **paneer cheese** or Homemade Paneer (page 260), optional

½ cup (125 mL) **vegetable broth**

CURRY SAUCE:

2 tbsp (30 mL) **vegetable oil**

2 **onions,** finely chopped (about 2 cups/500 mL)

1 tbsp (15 mL) minced **fresh ginger**

2 large cloves **garlic,** minced

2 **green finger chilies,** seeded and minced

1 tsp (5 mL) **ground coriander**

1 tsp (5 mL) **ground cumin**

1 tsp (5 mL) **garam masala**

¼ tsp (1 mL) **turmeric**

1 can (28 oz/796 mL) **diced tomatoes**

½ tsp (2 mL) **salt**

¼ cup (60 mL) chopped **fresh coriander**

CURRY SAUCE: In large shallow Dutch oven, heat oil over medium heat; fry onions, stirring often, until deep golden and softened, about 20 minutes.

Add ginger, garlic and chilies; cook, stirring, until fragrant, about 2 minutes. Add coriander, cumin, garam masala and turmeric; cook until fragrant and mixture sticks to pan, about 2 minutes. Add ¼ cup (60 mL) water; bring to boil, stirring and scraping up brown bits from bottom of pan.

Add tomatoes, salt and 1 cup (250 mL) water; bring to boil. Reduce heat and simmer until reduced to about 2½ cups (625 mL), about 15 minutes. Stir in coriander.

Add squash, green beans, carrots, paneer (if using), and broth; simmer, covered and stirring occasionally, until vegetables are tender, about 15 minutes.

* Garam masala is available in Indian stores and the spice aisle of many grocery stores and supermarkets. To make your own: In dry small skillet over medium heat, toast 1 each cinnamon stick and black cardamom pod, broken; 1 tsp (5 mL) each whole cloves and black peppercorns; and ½ tsp (2 mL) fennel seeds until fragrant. Grind in spice grinder until powdered. Makes about 1 tbsp (15 mL).

PER EACH OF 6 SERVINGS: about 122 cal, 3 g pro, 5 g total fat (trace sat. fat), 19 g carb, 4 g fibre, 0 mg chol, 462 mg sodium. % RDI: 9% calcium, 16% iron, 81% vit A, 52% vit C, 15% folate.

Grilled Corn Polenta with Roasted Red Peppers

Prep: 20 minutes **Stand:** 45 minutes **Cook:** 35 minutes **Makes:** 12 servings

¾ tsp (4 mL) **salt**

1 cup (250 mL) **cornmeal**

1 cup (250 mL) **fresh corn kernels**

½ cup (125 mL) grated **Parmesan cheese**

ROASTED RED PEPPERS:

3 **sweet red peppers**

1 tbsp (15 mL) **extra-virgin olive oil**

1 tsp (5 mL) **white wine vinegar**

Pinch **salt**

8 large **fresh basil leaves**

ROASTED RED PEPPERS: Broil (or grill over medium-high heat) red peppers, turning often, until charred and tender, about 15 minutes. Transfer to bowl; let stand, covered, for 15 minutes. Uncover and, once cool enough to handle, peel, core, seed and thinly slice; return to bowl. Sprinkle with oil, vinegar and salt; toss to combine.

In large saucepan, bring 4 cups (1 L) water and salt to boil; reduce heat to low. Gradually whisk in cornmeal; cook, stirring often with wooden spoon, for 10 minutes.

Stir in corn; cook until tender-crisp and polenta is thick enough to mound on spoon, 5 to 10 minutes. Stir in cheese.

Spread in greased 13- x 9-inch (3 L) glass baking dish. Let cool until set, about 30 minutes.

Cut polenta into 12 squares. Grill on greased grill over medium heat, turning once, until grill marked and hot, about 5 minutes. Thinly slice basil; stir into Roasted Red Peppers. Spoon over polenta.

PER SERVING: about 90 cal, 3 g pro, 3 g total fat (1 g sat. fat), 14 g carb, 2 g fibre, 4 mg chol, 114 mg sodium, 100 mg potassium. % RDI: 5% calcium, 3% iron, 12% vit A, 83% vit C, 15% folate.

Summer Vegetable Tian

Prep: 10 minutes   **Cook:** 2½ hours   **Makes:** 4 servings

¼ cup (60 mL) **olive oil**

1 **Spanish onion,** thinly sliced

¾ tsp (4 mL) **salt**

½ tsp (2 mL) **pepper**

2 cloves **garlic,** minced

¼ cup (60 mL) **fresh basil leaves,**
   thinly sliced

2 tsp (10 mL) chopped **fresh thyme**

2 **Japanese eggplants**
   (about 10 oz/300 g)

1 large **zucchini** (about 10 oz/
   300 g)

5 **plum tomatoes**

2 tsp (10 mL) **balsamic vinegar**

* Sprinkle this colourful ratatouille-style baked dish with Parmesan cheese shavings or crumbled goat cheese if desired.

In skillet, heat half of the oil over medium heat; fry onion, ½ tsp (2 mL) of the salt and half of the pepper, stirring often, until onion is very soft and caramelized, about 18 minutes. Add garlic, half of the basil and the thyme; cook for 2 minutes. Spread evenly over bottom of 11- x 7-inch (2 L) baking dish.

Cut eggplants, zucchini and tomatoes into ¼-inch (5 mm) thick slices. Alternating vegetables and overlapping slices, lay tightly together in single layer over onions in concentric rings. Drizzle with remaining oil; sprinkle with remaining salt and pepper. Drizzle with vinegar.

Cover with foil; bake in 325°F (160°C) oven for 1 hour. Uncover and bake until vegetables are very soft, about 1 hour. Sprinkle with remaining basil.

VEGETABLES

PER SERVING: about 211 cal, 3 g pro, 14 g total fat (2 g sat. fat), 21 g carb, 5 g fibre, 0 mg chol, 441 mg sodium, 589 mg potassium. % RDI: 4% calcium, 9% iron, 15% vit A, 32% vit C, 19% folate.

Burani Bonjon

Prep: 30 minutes   **Cook:** 45 minutes   **Makes:** 8 servings

✳ Eggplant braised in spicy tomato sauce then smothered with mint-garlic yogurt sauce is a classic Afghan dish.

3 **eggplants** (3 lb/1.5 kg total)
⅓ cup (75 mL) **olive oil**
1 tsp (5 mL) each **salt** and **pepper**
1 **onion,** minced
3 cloves **garlic,** minced
1 can (28 oz/796 mL) **diced tomatoes,** drained
2 tbsp (30 mL) **tomato paste**
1 tsp (5 mL) **turmeric**

¼ tsp (1 mL) **cayenne pepper**
3 tbsp (45 mL) chopped **fresh coriander**

MINT-GARLIC YOGURT SAUCE:
2 cloves **garlic**
½ tsp (2 mL) **salt**
1 cup (250 mL) **Balkan-style plain yogurt**
2 tbsp (30 mL) chopped **fresh mint**

MINT-GARLIC YOGURT SAUCE: On cutting board and using side of knife, mash garlic with salt until smooth paste. Whisk together yogurt, garlic paste and all but 2 tsp (10 mL) of the mint.

Cut eggplants into ½-inch (1 cm) thick rounds. Whisk ¼ cup (60 mL) of the oil with ½ tsp (2 mL) each of the salt and pepper; brush over eggplant slices. Arrange in single layer on foil-lined rimmed baking sheets; broil, 1 sheet at a time, turning once, until softened, browned and edges are wrinkled, about 10 minutes.

Meanwhile, in skillet, heat remaining oil over medium-high heat; fry onion and garlic until golden, about 5 minutes. Add tomatoes, tomato paste, turmeric, cayenne, and remaining salt and pepper; bring to boil. Reduce heat and simmer until sauce is thick, about 8 minutes.

Arrange half of the eggplant in greased 13- x 9-inch (3 L) glass baking dish; top with 1 cup (250 mL) of the tomato sauce. Top with remaining eggplant, then remaining tomato sauce. Sprinkle with 2 tbsp (30 mL) of the coriander.

Bake in 375°F (190°C) oven until bubbly, about 25 minutes. Let cool for 15 minutes. To serve, pour Mint-Garlic Yogurt Sauce over eggplant; sprinkle with remaining mint and coriander.

PER SERVING: about 169 cal, 4 g pro, 10 g total fat (2 g sat. fat), 18 g carb, 5 g fibre, 3 mg chol, 556 mg sodium. % RDI: 8% calcium, 10% iron, 7% vit A, 27% vit C, 16% folate.

Golden Onion Tart

Prep: 18 minutes   **Cook:** 45 minutes   **Makes:** 4 to 6 servings

2 tbsp (30 mL) **olive oil**

6 cups (1.5 L) sliced **sweet onions** (about 2½ lb/1.25 kg)

¼ tsp (1 mL) **caraway seeds**

2 tbsp (30 mL) **white wine vinegar** or sherry vinegar

¾ tsp (4 mL) each **salt** and **pepper**

2 cloves **garlic,** minced

1 lb (500 g) **pizza dough**, at room temperature, or homemade Pizza Dough (page 268)

1 **egg,** beaten

⅓ cup (75 mL) **sour cream**

1 **green onion,** chopped

✳ As easy to make as a pizza, this Alsatian-inspired tart is smothered in golden onions and garlic. Enjoy it warm or at room temperature.

In shallow Dutch oven, heat oil over medium heat; fry sliced onions, stirring occasionally, until soft and golden, 12 to 15 minutes.

Meanwhile, using mortar and pestle or bottom of heavy skillet, crush caraway seeds; add to pan along with vinegar, salt, pepper and garlic. Cook, scraping up any brown bits from bottom of pan, for 1 minute. Scrape into large bowl; let cool slightly.

On lightly floured surface, stretch or roll out dough to 14-inch (35 cm) circle. Place on greased 12-inch (30 cm) pizza pan. Roll up overhang to form lip, pinching to seal.

Add egg, sour cream and green onion to cooked onion mixture; mix well. Spread evenly over dough, leaving lip uncovered. Bake in 350°F (180°C) oven until crust is golden and filling is set in centre, about 30 minutes. Let stand for 5 minutes before cutting into wedges.

VEGETABLES

PER EACH OF 6 SERVINGS: about 341 cal, 9 g pro, 11 g total fat (3 g sat. fat), 53 g carb, 4 g fibre, 39 mg chol, 671 mg sodium. % RDI: 7% calcium, 17% iron, 3% vit A, 13% vit C, 23% folate.

Sweet Potato Strudel with Balsamic Mushroom Sauce

Prep: 30 minutes   **Stand:** 20 minutes   **Cook:** 50 minutes   **Makes:** 12 servings

1 tbsp (15 mL) **olive oil**

2 **sweet onions,** sliced

3 cloves **garlic,** sliced

1 tbsp (15 mL) chopped **fresh thyme**

1 tsp (5 mL) **salt**

½ tsp (2 mL) **pepper**

5 cups (1.25 L) **cremini,** white or oyster **mushrooms,** sliced

10 cups (2.5 L) thinly sliced peeled **sweet potatoes** (3 or 4 large)

2 tbsp (30 mL) chopped **fresh parsley**

1 tbsp (15 mL) **balsamic vinegar**

8 sheets **phyllo pastry,** thawed

½ cup (125 mL) **butter,** melted

2 tbsp (30 mL) **whole parsley leaves**

BALSAMIC MUSHROOM SAUCE:

1 pkg (½ oz/14 g) **dried porcini mushrooms**

1½ cups (375 mL) **boiling water**

1 tbsp (15 mL) **olive oil** or butter

1 tsp (5 mL) chopped **fresh thyme**

¼ tsp (1 mL) each **salt** and **pepper**

4 tsp (20 mL) **all-purpose flour**

1 tbsp (15 mL) **balsamic vinegar**

In large Dutch oven, heat oil over medium heat; fry onions, garlic, thyme, salt and pepper, stirring often, until golden, about 10 minutes. Add mushrooms; fry until softened, about 5 minutes. Add sweet potatoes and ¼ cup (60 mL) water; simmer, covered and stirring often, until potatoes are tender, about 10 minutes. Stir in chopped parsley and vinegar. Let cool to room temperature, about 20 minutes.

Lay 1 sheet of the phyllo on work surface, covering remainder with damp cloth. Brush lightly with butter; arrange half of the whole parsley leaves over phyllo. Top with 3 sheets phyllo, brushing first 2 with butter.

Spoon half of the potato mixture along 1 long side of phyllo, leaving 2-inch (5 cm) border at each end. Fold ends over filling; roll up. Place on large parchment paper–lined rimmed baking sheet. Brush all over with half of the remaining butter. With sharp knife, score top diagonally through phyllo into 6 servings. Repeat with remaining ingredients to make second roll. (To store and bake later, cover with plastic wrap; refrigerate for up to 24 hours. Add 10 minutes to baking time.)

Bake in 400°F (200°C) oven until golden, about 20 minutes. With serrated knife and using score marks as guides, cut into slices.

BALSAMIC MUSHROOM SAUCE: Meanwhile, soak mushrooms in boiling water for 20 minutes. Reserving soaking liquid, drain; squeeze out liquid from mushrooms. Pat dry.

In small saucepan, heat oil over medium heat; fry mushrooms, thyme, salt and pepper, stirring often, until softened, about 2 minutes. Stir in flour; cook, stirring, for 1 minute. Stir in reserved soaking liquid; bring to boil. Reduce heat and simmer until thickened, about 2 minutes. Stir in vinegar. Serve with strudel.

PER SERVING: about 242 cal, 4 g pro, 11 g total fat (5 g sat. fat), 33 g carb, 3 g fibre, 24 mg chol, 413 mg sodium. % RDI: 4% calcium, 11% iron, 121% vit A, 25% vit C, 17% folate.

Baked Eggplant Parmigiana with Marinara Sauce

Prep: 15 minutes   **Cook:** 18 minutes   **Makes:** 4 servings

½ cup (125 mL) **dry bread crumbs**

2 tbsp (30 mL) grated **Parmesan cheese** (approx)

1 tbsp (15 mL) chopped **fresh oregano**

½ cup (125 mL) **all-purpose flour**

2 **eggs,** lightly beaten

1 **eggplant** (about 1 lb/500 g)

2 tbsp (30 mL) **olive oil**

1½ cups (375 mL) **Marinara Sauce** (page 271)

Thinly sliced fresh basil

In shallow dish, combine bread crumbs, Parmesan cheese and oregano. Place flour in second shallow dish and eggs in third. Cut eggplant into ½-inch (1 cm) thick rounds; coat lightly in flour. Coat in eggs then crumb mixture.

Place on greased foil-lined baking sheet; drizzle with oil. Bake in 400°F (200°C) oven, turning once, until tender inside, and crispy and golden outside, 18 to 20 minutes. Serve topped with warmed Marinara Sauce. Sprinkle with basil, and more cheese if desired.

VEGETABLES

PER SERVING: about 325 cal, 10 g pro, 15 g total fat (3 g sat. fat), 40 g carb, 6 g fibre, 96 mg chol, 582 mg sodium. % RDI: 14% calcium, 29% iron, 7% vit A, 48% vit C, 39% folate.

Savoy Cabbage & Swiss Cheese Bake

Prep: 20 minutes   **Cook:** 1 hour   **Makes:** 6 servings

⅓ cup (75 mL) **olive oil**

1 large **onion,** thinly sliced

4 cloves **garlic,** minced

10 cups (2.5 L) shredded **savoy cabbage** (about 1 head, 2 lb/1 kg)

1 tsp (5 mL) **salt**

½ tsp (2 mL) **pepper**

½ cup (125 mL) **dry white wine** or vegetable broth

1 loaf (8 oz/250 g) **crusty white** or multigrain **bread**

2 cups (500 mL) shredded **Swiss cheese**

½ cup (125 mL) grated **Parmesan cheese**

In shallow Dutch oven, heat 3 tbsp (45 mL) of the oil over medium heat; fry onion and half of the garlic until onion is softened, about 5 minutes. Add cabbage, salt and pepper; cook, stirring often, until wilted and golden, about 15 minutes. Add wine; cook until cabbage is very soft, about 10 minutes.

Meanwhile, cut bread into ¾-inch (2 cm) thick slices; place on baking sheet. Toast in 400°F (200°C) oven, turning once, until golden and dry, about 10 minutes. Let cool. Cut remaining cloves of garlic in half; rub cut sides all over each slice of bread.

Line 13- x 9-inch (3 L) glass baking dish with half of the bread slices, fitting to cover bottom. Top with half of the cabbage, then half each of the Swiss and Parmesan cheeses. Repeat layers once. Carefully pour 8 cups (2 L) hot water along edge of dish into casserole; drizzle with remaining oil.

Bake in 350°F (180°C) oven until bubbly and cheese is golden, about 30 minutes. Cut into squares; serve in shallow bowls with some of the broth.

✳ Slow-cooked cabbage becomes sweet and caramelized in this rustic brothy bread pudding. Serve in wide shallow bowls, passing additional Parmesan cheese, if desired.

VEGETABLES

PER SERVING: about 432 cal, 19 g pro, 26 g total fat (10 g sat. fat), 32 g carb, 5 g fibre, 40 mg chol, 849 mg sodium, 383 mg potassium. % RDI: 42% calcium, 14% iron, 21% vit A, 38% vit C, 44% folate.

STOCKS, SAUCES, BREADS & BASICS

Simple Soda Bread
(page 266)

Roasted Vegetable Stock

Prep: 5 minutes   **Cook:** 1¾ hours   **Makes:** about 5 cups (1.25 L)

3 **carrots,** coarsely chopped

3 **onions,** coarsely chopped

3 stalks **celery,** coarsely chopped

1 cup (250 mL) sliced **mushrooms**
 (stems or caps)

3 cloves **garlic**

2 tsp (10 mL) **vegetable oil**

10 sprigs **fresh parsley**

10 black **peppercorns,** cracked

2 **bay leaves**

8 cups (2 L) **cold water**

½ tsp (2 mL) **salt**

In large roasting pan, stir together carrots, onions, celery, mushrooms, garlic and oil to coat. Roast in 450°F (230°C) oven, stirring halfway through, until softened and browned, about 40 minutes. Transfer to stockpot.

Add parsley, peppercorns, bay leaves and all but 1 cup (250 mL) of the water to stockpot. Pour remaining water into roasting pan, stirring and scraping up brown bits from bottom of pan, over heat if necessary. Scrape into stockpot; bring to boil. Skim off any foam. Reduce heat to medium; simmer until flavourful, about 1 hour.

Strain through fine sieve, gently pressing vegetables. Stir in salt. (To store, let cool for 30 minutes; refrigerate in airtight container for up to 3 days or freeze for up to 4 months.)

✳ Richly flavoured and coloured, this stock wonderful in soups, such as Potato Mushroom Goulash (page 214) and Tomato Peanut Soup (page 152). For even deeper flavour, add a couple of dried shiitake mushrooms when the stock is simmering.

STOCKS, SAUCES, BREADS & BASICS

PER ½ CUP (125 ML): about 33 cal, 1 g pro, 1 g total fat (0 g sat. fat), 5 g carb, 0 g fibre, 0 mg chol, 145 mg sodium. % RDI: 2% calcium, 4% iron, 57% vit A, 13% vit C, 8% folate.

Homemade Vegetable Stock

Prep: 5 minutes   **Cook:** 1½ hours   **Makes:** 8 cups (2 L)

3 **plum tomatoes,** halved

3 **carrots** (unpeeled), coarsely chopped

3 **onions** (unpeeled), coarsely chopped

3 stalks **celery** with leaves, coarsely chopped

1 head **garlic** (unpeeled), broken into cloves

2 **bay leaves**

6 sprigs **fresh parsley**

5 sprigs **fresh thyme**

10 **black peppercorns**

10 cups (2.5 L) **cold water**

½ tsp (2 mL) **salt** (optional)

In stockpot, combine tomatoes, carrots, onions, celery, garlic, bay leaves, parsley, thyme and peppercorns; pour in water.

Bring to boil; reduce heat and simmer until flavourful, about 1½ hours.

Strain through fine sieve, gently pressing vegetables. Stir in salt, if using. (To store, let cool for 30 minutes; refrigerate in airtight container for up to 3 days or freeze for up to 4 months.)

STOCKS, SAUCES, BREADS & BASICS

PER ½ CUP (125 ML): about 1 cal, 0 g pro, 1 g total fat (0 g sat. fat), trace carb, 0 g fibre, 0 mg chol, 0 mg sodium. % RDI: 1% folate.

TAKING STOCK

Stock is a key ingredient in any cook's kitchen.
It's the ideal base for soups, sauces and stews,
and cooking rice or other grains in stock adds
a big flavour boost.

Your own homemade stock is much more delicious than store-bought, and it's also very frugal. Think of stock making as an opportunity to extract flavour from not just whole vegetables but also from their otherwise unused trimmings. Leek tops, celery leaves, shiitake stems and fresh herb stems are some of our favourite trimmings.

While we strongly encourage you to keep a supply of homemade stock on hand (as well as a container or resealable bag in the freezer for collecting vegetable trimmings), we know it isn't always convenient. So, in many of our recipes, we suggest using store-bought vegetable broth – the type sold in Tetra Paks is our second choice when homemade is unavailable.

If you find yourself thinking the sodium content seems high on a recipe that calls for commercial vegetable broth that's the culprit. We hope that sodium-reduced versions will find their way to store shelves in the near future. If you use homemade stock, you control how much salt you add and can reduce your sodium intake drastically. Or combine store-bought vegetable broth with water to cut the salt.

For a lighter, pure-flavoured vegetable stock, our Homemade Vegetable Stock (opposite) is what you're after. For a more intensely flavoured one, try Roasted Vegetable Stock (page 255).

STOCKS, SAUCES, BREADS & BASICS

Homemade Ricotta

Prep: 5 minutes **Stand:** 50 minutes **Cook:** 40 minutes
Makes: 2 cups (500 mL)

* Slightly higher in fat than homogenized milk, organic whole milk is best for this recipe because it has rich flavour. This cheese is fantastic still-warm with just a drizzle of honey, a few berries and some cracked black pepper. It's also lovely in Spaghettini with Homemade Ricotta & Herbs (page 94).

8 cups (2 L) **organic whole milk**
  (3.8% MF)
½ tsp (2 mL) **salt**
5 tbsp (75 mL) **white vinegar**

In large heavy-bottomed saucepan, heat milk with salt over medium-low heat, stirring often, until temperature reaches 203°F (95°C), about 40 minutes.

Add vinegar; stir slowly 3 times. Remove from heat; let stand for 20 minutes.

With skimmer or slotted spoon, gently skim off curds into sieve lined with double-thickness cheesecloth. Let drain for 30 minutes. Transfer to serving bowl. (Or, refrigerate for up to 2 days.)

PER 1 TBSP (15 ML): about 25 cal, 2 g pro, 2 g total fat (1 g sat. fat), 1 g carb, trace fibre, 7 mg chol, 19 mg sodium, 18 mg potassium. % RDI: 5% calcium, 1% vit A, 1% folate.

Homemade Paneer

Prep: 5 minutes   **Stand:** 8½ hours   **Cook:** 6 minutes
Makes: about 1 lb (500 g)

✳ Paneer, often used in Indian cooking, is fresh, unripened cheese made by curdling whole milk to separate the curds from the whey. If you can't find it in a store, this recipe shows you how easy it is to make your own. Use in Spinach & Rapini Curry with Paneer (page 202) and Vegetable Curry with Squash (page 241).

12 cups (3 L) **homogenized milk**
1 cup (250 mL) **lemon juice**
¼ tsp (1 mL) **salt**

In large heavy-bottomed saucepan, bring milk to boil; remove from heat. Add lemon juice; stir until milk curdles and separates into spongy white chunks (curds) and greenish milky water (whey). Stir in salt.

Line sieve with double-thickness cheesecloth; set over bowl. Strain mixture; let stand until most of the liquid is drained off.

Fold cheesecloth over top; weigh down with plate and full 28-oz (796 mL) can. Refrigerate for 8 hours or up to 24 hours. Remove cheese from cheesecloth. (Or, refrigerate in airtight container for up to 5 days.)

PER 2 OZ (60 G): about 161 cal, 10 g pro, 11 g total fat (7 g sat. fat), 6 g carb, 0 g fibre, 45 mg chol, 118 mg sodium, 163 mg potassium. % RDI: 29% calcium, 9% vit A, 12% vit C, 7% folate.

Three-Seed Biscuits

Prep: 25 minutes   **Cook:** 12 minutes   **Makes:** 12 biscuits

1¼ cups (300 mL) **all-purpose flour**

1 cup (250 mL) **whole wheat flour**

¼ cup (60 mL) **sunflower seeds**

¼ cup (60 mL) **flaxseeds**

¼ cup (60 mL) **wheat germ**

1 tbsp (15 mL) **granulated sugar**

1 tbsp (15 mL) **baking powder**

½ tsp (2 mL) **salt**

½ cup (125 mL) cold **butter,** cubed

1 cup (250 mL) **milk**

1 **egg,** lightly beaten

2 tbsp (30 mL) **sesame seeds**

⁎ Quick and easy to assemble and bake, these biscuit fingers are wonderful with soups, such as Roasted Red Pepper & Sweet Potato Soup (page 211), and stews. Or enjoy them as a snack with honey or hummus.

Whisk together all-purpose and whole wheat flours, sunflower seeds, flaxseeds, wheat germ, sugar, baking powder and salt. Using pastry blender or 2 knives, cut in butter until in coarse crumbs. Stir in milk to form soft slightly sticky dough.

With floured hands, turn out onto lightly floured surface; knead gently 10 times. Pat out to 7-inch (18 cm) square. Cut into quarters; cut each quarter into 3 strips. Place, 1 inch (2.5 cm) apart, on ungreased baking sheet. Brush tops with egg; sprinkle with sesame seeds.

Bake in centre of 425°F (220°C) oven until golden, about 12 minutes. Let cool on pan on rack.

PER BISCUIT: about 225 cal, 6 g pro, 13 g total fat (6 g sat. fat), 23 g carb, 3 g fibre, 37 mg chol, 242 mg sodium. % RDI: 8% calcium, 13% iron, 8% vit A, 25% folate.

STOCKS, SAUCES, BREADS & BASICS

Rye Cracker Bread

Prep: 20 minutes   **Stand:** 10 minutes   **Cook:** 20 minutes
Makes: about 40 pieces

¾ cup (175 mL) **rye flour**
¾ cup (175 mL) **all-purpose flour**
¼ cup (60 mL) **flaxseeds**
¼ cup (60 mL) **ground flaxseeds**

4 tsp (20 mL) **butter,** softened
½ tsp (2 mL) **baking powder**
½ tsp (2 mL) **salt**
½ cup (125 mL) **milk**

In large bowl and using electric beater, beat together rye and all-purpose flours, flaxseeds, ground flaxseeds, butter, baking powder and salt until crumbly. Mix in milk until dough is pliable, soft and sticky, adding up to 3 tbsp (45 mL) water, 1 tbsp (15 mL) at a time, if necessary.

Turn out onto lightly floured surface; knead just until smooth. Wrap; let stand for 10 minutes.

Divide dough into quarters. On lightly floured surface, roll out, one-quarter at a time, to ⅛-inch (3 mm) thick 10-inch (25 cm) square. Place on ungreased rimless baking sheets.

Bake, 2 sheets at a time, in top and bottom thirds of 325°F (160°C) oven, rotating and switching pans halfway through, until golden and crisp, about 20 minutes. Let cool on rack; break into pieces. (To store, keep in airtight container for up to 1 week or freeze for up to 1 month.)

✱ This cracker bread, often called *lavash,* tastes better and is a lot cheaper than store-bought. Use a clean coffee grinder or mini chopper to grind your own flaxseeds: 3 tbsp (45 mL) seeds will yield about ¼ cup (60 mL) ground. For a different version, replace rye flour with whole-grain flour or whole wheat flour.

STOCKS, SAUCES, BREADS & BASICS

PER PIECE: about 29 cal, 1 g pro, 1 g total fat (trace sat. fat), 4 g carb, 1 g fibre, 1 mg chol, 38 mg sodium. % RDI: 1% calcium, 2% iron, 1% vit A, 4% folate.

Cheddar Herbed Skillet Cornbread

Prep: 10 minutes **Stand:** 5 minutes **Cook:** 30 minutes
Makes: 8 to 12 servings

* No multigrain flour? Use ⅓ cup (75 mL) each all-purpose and whole wheat flour. For additional flavour and colour, stir in ¼ cup (60 mL) chopped reconstituted (or drained oil-packed) sun-dried tomatoes.

1¾ cups (425 mL) **medium-grind cornmeal**
⅔ cup (150 mL) **multigrain flour**
1 tbsp (15 mL) **granulated sugar**
2 tsp (10 mL) **baking powder**
½ tsp (2 mL) **salt**
2 **eggs**

1½ cups (375 mL) **milk**
1 cup (250 mL) shredded **old Cheddar cheese**
1 tbsp (15 mL) chopped **fresh sage** or rosemary
2 tbsp (30 mL) **butter**

Heat 10-inch (25 cm) ovenproof cast-iron skillet in 450°F (230°C) oven until hot, about 5 minutes.

Meanwhile, whisk together cornmeal, flour, sugar, baking powder and salt. Beat eggs until foamy; whisk in milk. Pour over cornmeal mixture. Add half of the cheese and the sage; stir just until combined.

Add butter to hot pan, swirling to coat bottom and side. Scrape in batter; sprinkle with remaining cheese.

Bake until golden and firm to the touch, about 25 minutes. Let cool in pan on rack for 5 minutes. If desired, invert onto rack; invert top side up. (To make ahead of time, store in airtight container for up to 2 days or wrap in plastic wrap and freeze in airtight container for up to 2 weeks.)

PER EACH OF 12 SERVINGS: about 188 cal, 7 g pro, 7 g total fat (4 g sat. fat), 24 g carb, 2 g fibre, 48 mg chol, 242 mg sodium. % RDI: 12% calcium, 6% iron, 8% vit A, 20% folate.

Green Onion & Cheddar Scones

Prep: 20 minutes   **Cook:** 15 minutes   **Makes:** 12 scones

2½ cups (625 mL) **all-purpose flour**

1 tbsp (15 mL) **baking powder**

½ tsp (2 mL) **salt**

¼ tsp (1 mL) **cayenne pepper**

½ cup (125 mL) cold **butter,** cubed

1 cup (250 mL) shredded **extra-old Cheddar cheese**

¼ cup (60 mL) minced **green onions**

1 **egg**

1 cup (250 mL) **milk**

Whisk together flour, baking powder, salt and cayenne pepper. Using pastry blender or 2 knives, cut in butter until in coarse crumbs. Stir in ¾ cup (175 mL) of the cheese and green onions. Beat egg with milk; pour over flour mixture and stir with fork to form soft ragged dough. With lightly floured hands, press into ball.

Turn out onto lightly floured surface; knead gently 10 times. Pat into ¾-inch (2 cm) thick round. Using 2½-inch (6 cm) floured round cutter and pressing scraps together, cut out 12 rounds. Place on parchment paper–lined or floured rimless baking sheet. Sprinkle with remaining cheese.

Bake in centre of 400°F (200°C) oven until golden, about 15 minutes. (To store, let cool. Store in airtight container for up to 24 hours or wrap individually in plastic wrap and freeze in airtight container for up to 2 weeks.)

✱ Quick to make, golden and tender cheese-infused scones are terrific with soups or stews, or stuffed with a fried egg and sliced tomato for grab-and-go breakfast sandwiches. Or enjoy them on their own.

STOCKS, SAUCES, BREADS & BASICS

PER SCONE: about 219 cal, 6 g pro, 12 g total fat (7 g sat. fat), 22 g carb, 1 g fibre, 51 mg chol, 313 mg sodium. % RDI: 12% calcium, 10% iron, 12% vit A, 17% folate.

Simple Soda Bread

Prep: 12 minutes **Cook:** 35 minutes **Makes:** 4 servings

1 cup (250 mL) **all-purpose flour**
1 cup (250 mL) **whole wheat flour**
1 tbsp (15 mL) **granulated sugar**
2 tsp (10 mL) **baking powder**
½ tsp (2 mL) **baking soda**
¼ tsp (1 mL) **salt**

¼ cup (60 mL) **dried currants**
½ tsp (2 mL) **caraway seeds**
  (optional)
¾ cup (175 mL) **buttermilk**
3 tbsp (45 mL) **butter,** melted
1 **egg**

Whisk together all-purpose and whole wheat flours, sugar, baking powder and soda, and salt; stir in currants, and caraway seeds (if using).

Whisk together buttermilk, butter and egg; pour over flour mixture, tossing with fork to form sticky dough.

Turn out onto lightly floured surface; knead gently 10 times. Transfer to parchment paper–lined baking sheet; press into 7-inch (18 cm) round. With sharp knife, score into 8 wedges.

Bake in 350°F (180°C) oven until cake tester inserted in centre comes out clean, about 35 minutes.

PER SERVING: about 376 cal, 11 g pro, 12 g total fat (7 g sat. fat), 59 g carb, 5 g fibre, 73 mg chol, 571 mg sodium, 341 mg potassium. % RDI: 15% calcium, 23% iron, 10% vit A, 2% vit C, 37% folate.

Multigrain Pizza Dough

Prep: 15 minutes   **Stand:** 1 hour   **Makes:** about 1½ lb (750 g) dough, enough for one 14-inch (35 cm) pizza

1¾ cups (425 mL) **multigrain bread flour**

1½ cups (375 mL) **all-purpose flour**

¼ cup (60 mL) **mixed seeds** (such as flax, sunflower and sesame)

2 tsp (10 mL) **quick-rising (instant) dry yeast**

1 tsp (5 mL) **salt**

1¼ cups (300 mL) **hot water** (120°F/50°C)

1 tbsp (15 mL) **extra-virgin olive oil**

✳ Use as a base for Mushroom Fontina Pizza (page 187) or substitute for any recipe calling for regular pizza dough.

Combine multigrain and all-purpose flours, seeds, yeast and salt. With wooden spoon, gradually stir in water and oil to form ragged dough, using hands if necessary.

Turn out onto lightly floured surface; knead until smooth and elastic, about 8 minutes.

Place in greased bowl, turning to grease all over. Wrap; let rise in warm draft-free place until doubled in bulk, about 1 hour. (Or, refrigerate unrisen dough and let rise for 24 hours. Or freeze in plastic bag for up to 1 month; let thaw and rise in refrigerator overnight.)

VARIATION

BREAD MACHINE MULTIGRAIN PIZZA DOUGH: Into pan of 2-lb (1 kg) machine, place (in order) water, oil, salt, multigrain and all-purpose flours, seeds and yeast. (Do not let yeast touch liquid.) Choose dough setting.

STOCKS, SAUCES, BREADS & BASICS

Pizza Dough

Prep: 15 minutes   **Stand:** 1 hour   **Makes:** about 1½ lb (750 g) dough, enough for one 14-inch (35 cm) pizza

✳ The dough for this crisp, airy crust is easy to work – especially after 24 hours, because the gluten is relaxed and it rolls well. Use for Onion & Gorgonzola Pizza with Arugula (page 188), Golden Onion Tart (page 247) or Pizza Margherita (page 191).

3 cups (750 mL) **all-purpose flour** (approx)

2 tsp (10 mL) **quick-rising (instant) dry yeast**

1 tsp (5 mL) **salt**

1¼ cups (300 mL) **hot water** (120°F/50°C)

1 tbsp (15 mL) **extra-virgin olive oil**

Combine 2¾ cups (675 mL) of the flour, yeast and salt. With wooden spoon, gradually stir in water and oil to form ragged dough, using hands if necessary.

Turn out onto lightly floured surface; knead until smooth and elastic, about 8 minutes, adding up to ¼ cup (60 mL) more flour, 1 tbsp (15 mL) at a time, if necessary.

Place in greased bowl, turning to grease all over. Wrap; let rise in warm draft-free place until doubled in bulk, about 1 hour. (Or, refrigerate unrisen dough and let rise for 24 hours. Or freeze in plastic bag for up to 1 month; let thaw and rise in refrigerator overnight.)

VARIATION

BREAD MACHINE PIZZA DOUGH: Into pan of 2-lb (1 kg) machine, place (in order) water, oil, salt, flour and yeast. (Do not let yeast touch liquid.) Choose dough setting.

Tomato Pizza Sauce

Prep: 5 minutes   **Stand:** 5 minutes   **Cook:** 25 minutes
Makes: 2 cups (500 mL)

✳ Homemade tomato pizza sauce is much more flavourful than the commercial variety. This makes enough for two pizzas and doubles easily for more.

1 can (28 oz/796 mL) **whole tomatoes**
2 tbsp (30 mL) **extra-virgin olive oil**
1 small **onion,** minced
2 cloves **garlic,** minced

¼ tsp (1 mL) **dried oregano**
½ tsp (2 mL) **wine vinegar**
Pinch each **salt** and **pepper**
Pinch **granulated sugar**

Reserving juice, drain, seed and chop tomatoes.

In saucepan, heat oil over medium heat; fry onion, garlic and oregano, stirring occasionally, until onion is softened, about 5 minutes.

Add tomatoes and reserved juice, vinegar, salt, pepper and sugar; simmer until thickened, about 20 minutes. Let cool for 5 minutes.

Transfer to food processor; blend until smooth. (To store, refrigerate in airtight container for up to 1 week or freeze for up to 1 month.)

PER ½ CUP (125 mL): about 101 cal, 2 g pro, 7 g total fat (1 g sat. fat), 10 g carb, 2 g fibre, 0 mg chol, 239 mg sodium, 382 mg potassium. % RDI: 6% calcium, 14% iron, 2% vit A, 43% vit C, 6% folate.

Marinara Sauce

Prep: 8 minutes   **Stand:** 10 minutes   **Cook:** 50 minutes
Makes: about 5 cups (1.25 L)

2 tbsp (30 mL) **extra-virgin olive oil**

4 cloves **garlic**

2 cans (each 28 oz/796 mL) **whole tomatoes**

1 tbsp (15 mL) **balsamic vinegar**

Pinch **salt**

Pinch **granulated sugar**

Pinch **hot pepper flakes**

1 sprig (about 8 leaves) **fresh basil**

In saucepan, heat oil over medium heat; fry garlic, stirring often, until golden, about 3 minutes.

Add tomatoes, breaking up with back of spoon. Stir in vinegar, salt, sugar, hot pepper flakes and basil; bring to boil. Reduce heat and simmer, stirring occasionally, until thickened, about 45 minutes. Let cool slightly; discard basil.

In food processor or blender, purée sauce.

* Use this versatile herb-and-tomato sauce in Spinach & Rice Phyllo Pie (page 67), Spaghetti & Tofu Balls (page 125), Baked Eggplant Parmigiana with Marinara Sauce (page 250) and Tahini Carrot Tofu Patties (page 136). You can refrigerate the sauce for up to 3 days or freeze for up to 2 months.

STOCKS, SAUCES, BREADS & BASICS

PER ¼ CUP (60 mL): about 46 cal, 1 g pro, 2 g total fat (trace sat. fat), 6 g carb, 1 g fibre, 0 mg chol, 173 mg sodium. % RDI: 4% calcium, 10% iron, 2% vit A, 30% vit C, 4% folate.

Thai Green Curry Paste

Prep: 10 minutes   **Makes:** ¾ cup (175 mL)

✳ Use this all-purpose curry base in Thai Green Curry with Tofu & Vegetables (page 122).

5 **green chilies,** seeded and chopped

2 stalks **lemongrass,** finely chopped (or 2 tsp/10 mL lemongrass paste)

1 cup (250 mL) packed **fresh coriander** (with roots and stems)

¼ cup (60 mL) chopped **shallots**

2 tbsp (30 mL) minced **garlic**

2 tbsp (30 mL) grated **fresh ginger**

2 tsp (10 mL) grated **lime rind**

½ tsp (2 mL) **turmeric**

½ tsp (2 mL) **ground coriander**

½ tsp (2 mL) **ground cumin**

In blender, purée together chilies, lemongrass, fresh coriander, shallots, garlic, ginger, lime rind, turmeric, ground coriander and cumin, adding up to ¼ cup (60 mL) water if necessary to make smooth paste. (To store, refrigerate in airtight container for up to 2 weeks.)

PER 1 TBSP (15 mL): about 13 cal, trace pro, trace total fat (0 g sat. fat), 3 g carb, trace fibre, 0 mg chol, 2 mg sodium. % RDI: 1% calcium, 4% iron, 2% vit A, 5% vit C, 2% folate.

Spinach Raita

Prep: 5 minutes   **Stand:** 30 minutes   **Cook:** 8 minutes

Makes: about 1¾ cups (425 mL)

1½ cups (375 mL) **plain yogurt**

1 pkg (10 oz/284 g) **fresh spinach,** trimmed

¼ cup (60 mL) chopped **fresh mint** or coriander

¼ tsp (1 mL) grated **lemon rind**

3 tbsp (45 mL) **lemon juice**

½ tsp (2 mL) **salt**

¼ tsp (1 mL) **pepper**

2 tsp (10 mL) **black mustard seeds** (optional)

Drain yogurt in cheesecloth-lined sieve for 30 minutes.

Rinse spinach; shake off excess water. In large saucepan or Dutch oven over medium-high heat, cook spinach, covered and stirring once, just until wilted, 4 to 5 minutes. Drain and let cool enough to handle; squeeze out liquid. Chop finely. Mix together spinach, drained yogurt, mint, lemon rind and juice, salt and pepper.

In dry skillet, toast mustard seeds (if using) over medium heat just until seeds turn grey and crackle, about 3 minutes. Stir into yogurt mixture.

✳ Raita is best made with full-fat Balkan-style yogurt. You can use reduced-fat but not fat-free. Serve this as a cooling, refreshing condiment with Spiced Brown Rice Pilau with Eggplant (page 64) or Vegetable Biryani (page 68)

STOCKS, SAUCES, BREADS & BASICS

PER ¼ CUP (60 mL): about 64 cal, 3 g pro, 3 g total fat (2 g sat. fat), 6 g carb, 1 g fibre, 9 mg chol, 217 mg sodium. % RDI: 12% calcium, 11% iron, 35% vit A, 12% vit C, 28% folate.

Harissa

Prep: 5 minutes   **Stand:** 1 hour   **Cook:** 6 minutes   **Makes:** 2⅔ cups (650 mL)

1 tbsp (15 mL) **coriander seeds**

2 tsp (10 mL) **caraway seeds**

2 tsp (10 mL) **cumin seeds**

5 **dried hot red peppers,** seeded

½ cup (125 mL) **extra-virgin olive oil**

5 cloves **garlic,** peeled

2 jars (each 370 g) **roasted red peppers,** drained

2 tsp (10 mL) **granulated sugar**

¼ tsp (1 mL) each **salt** and **pepper**

In small dry skillet, toast coriander, caraway and cumin seeds and hot peppers over medium heat until fragrant, about 1 minute. With spice grinder, or in mortar with pestle, grind to fine powder; transfer to food processor.

In same skillet, heat half of the oil over low heat, fry garlic, turning occasionally, until deep golden, about 5 minutes. Scrape oil and garlic into food processor. Add roasted red peppers, remaining oil, sugar, salt and pepper; purée until smooth. Let stand for 1 hour before using. (Or, refrigerate for up to 1 week, or freeze for up to 2 months.)

✳ This North African sauce of chilies and garlic is fantastic as a condiment with Squash Couscous (page 63). If you like a fair amount of heat, leave in the hot pepper seeds.

STOCKS, SAUCES, BREADS & BASICS

PER 1 TBSP (15 mL): about 28 cal, trace pro, 3 g total fat (trace sat. fat), 1 g carb, trace fibre, 0 mg chol, 38 mg sodium, 25 mg potassium. % RDI: 1% iron, 4% vit A, 30% vit C, 1% folate.

Fresh Coriander Chutney

Prep: 5 minutes   **Makes:** ½ cup (125 mL)

* Great with any East Indian-inspired rice dish, this simple and fresh condiment was created to go with Vegetable Samosas (page 166). Be sure to wash the coriander well, as it is often quite sandy. Then, dry it in a salad spinner.

4 cups (1 L) **fresh coriander leaves**
Half **hot green finger pepper,**
   seeded
4 tsp (20 mL) **lemon juice**
¼ tsp (1 mL) **salt**

In food processor, purée together coriander, ¼ cup (60 mL) water, hot pepper, lemon juice and salt until smooth. (Refrigerate in airtight container for no more than 6 hours to avoid discolouration.)

PER 1 TBSP (15 mL): about 3 cal, trace pro, 0 g total fat (0 g sat. fat), 1 g carb, trace fibre, 0 mg chol, 76 mg sodium, 46 mg potassium. % RDI: 1% calcium, 1% iron, 6% vit A, 7% vit C. 2% folate.

Winter Fruit Chutney

Prep: 15 minutes   **Stand:** 30 minutes   **Cook:** 1 hour
Makes: about 2 cups (500 mL)

¾ cup (175 mL) chopped pitted **prunes**

¾ cup (175 mL) chopped **dried apricots**

1 **onion,** chopped

1 **Granny Smith apple,** peeled and finely chopped

½ cup (125 mL) chopped drained seeded **canned tomatoes**

⅓ cup (75 mL) **granulated sugar**

¼ cup (60 mL) **cider vinegar**

½ tsp (2 mL) **ground ginger**

¼ tsp (1 mL) **cinnamon**

¼ tsp (1 mL) **ground cloves**

¼ tsp (1 mL) **nutmeg**

¼ tsp (1 mL) **pepper**

¼ tsp (1 mL) **cayenne pepper**

¼ tsp (1 mL) **salt**

✳ A favourite accompaniment to tourtière, including Chestnut Tourtière (page 174), this chutney is also wonderful with cheese and crackers.

In saucepan, bring prunes, apricots and 1 cup (250 mL) water to boil. Remove from heat; let stand, covered, for 30 minutes.

Stir in onion, apple, tomatoes, sugar, vinegar, ginger, cinnamon, cloves, nutmeg, pepper, cayenne pepper and salt; bring to simmer. Simmer, covered and stirring occasionally, until thickened, 50 to 60 minutes. (To store, let cool; refrigerate in airtight container for up to 5 days.)

PER 2 TBSP (25 ML): about 60 cal, 1 g pro, trace total fat (0 g sat. fat), 16 g carb, 1 g fibre, 0 mg chol, 47 mg sodium. % RDI: 1% calcium, 3% iron, 3% vit A, 2% vit C, 1% folate.

STOCKS, SAUCES, BREADS & BASICS

Tomato Pear Chutney

Prep: 12 minutes **Cook:** 1¼ hours **Makes:** 1½ cups (375 mL)

＊ Savoury-sweet with a little kick of heat, this chunky sauce makes an ideal mate for any grilled cheese sandwich or savoury pie, especially our Vegetarian Tourtière (page 132).

1 cup (250 mL) diced seeded peeled **tomato**

1 **pear,** peeled, cored and diced

1 **jalapeño pepper,** minced

1 clove **garlic,** minced

¼ cup (60 mL) **golden raisins**

3 tbsp (45 mL) **cider vinegar**

2 tbsp (30 mL) packed **brown sugar**

1 tbsp (15 mL) **tomato paste**

1 **cinnamon stick**

1 **star anise**

¼ tsp (1 mL) each **salt** and **pepper**

In saucepan, combine tomato, pear, jalapeño, garlic, raisins, vinegar, brown sugar, tomato paste, cinnamon, star anise, salt, pepper and ⅓ cup (75 mL) water; bring to boil. Reduce heat and simmer, covered and stirring occasionally, for 45 minutes.

Discard cinnamon stick and star anise; simmer, uncovered, until thickened, about 20 minutes. (To store, let cool; refrigerate in airtight container for up to 5 days.)

PER 1 TBSP (15 mL): about 15 cal, trace pro, 0 g total fat (0 g sat. fat), 4 g carb, trace fibre, 0 mg chol, 26 mg sodium. % RDI: 1% iron, 1% vit A, 1% vit C.

ACKNOWLEDGMENTS

I am grateful to have had such a proficient and capable team of dedicated people involved in the creation and evolution of *The Vegetarian Collection*. First and foremost, I would like to thank my hero, our project editor, Tina Anson Mine, for navigating us all through the occasionally murky seas of this project. She provided editing expertise, helpful advice, suggestions and encouragement, made all the more enjoyable with her quick wit, her sense of humour and our shared admiration of Edward Gorey. Thanks also to copy editor Austen Gilliland for her thorough work in ensuring that each recipe is as accurate, clear and concise as can be, and to indexer Gillian Watts, who has made it as easy as veggie pie for you to find what you need in this book. Credit for the books nutritional analysis goes to Sharyn Joliat of Info Access.

A big thank-you to *Canadian Living*'s food editor, Gabrielle Bright, for entrusting me with this project, and to the past and present team of food specialists and recipe creators in The Canadian Living Test Kitchen. Special thanks go to our food editor-at-large, Christine Picheca, for her many scrumptious recipe contributions to this book. Editorial assistants Pat Flynn and Gia Antonacci assisted with the arduous task of pulling together materials and visuals.

The credit for the outstanding design of this book goes to the enormously talented and affable Chris Bond, who, along with creative director Michael Erb, brought all the visual elements of this tantalizing recipe collection to life. Thanks also to Felix Wedgwood, photographer extraordinaire, for all the gorgeous new photography. Food stylist Lucie Richard and prop stylist Laura Branson deftly worked with Felix to create many of these mouthwatering pictures.

Finally, much appreciation goes out to our peerless editor-in-chief, Susan Antonacci; group publisher, Lynn Chambers; Transcontinental Books publisher, Jean Paré; and Janet Joy Wilson and Duncan Shields of Random House Canada for their encouragement and belief in this project. This cookbook collection would not exist without you all.

– Alison Kent

INDEX

281

282

INDEX

INDEX

288

CREDITS

Recipes

All recipes were developed by **Alison Kent** and **The Canadian Living Test Kitchen,** except the following:

Andrew Chase, *Homemakers* Magazine: pages 37, 56, 64, 135 and 273.

Photography

Michael Alberstat: page 246.
Luis Albuquerque: page 138.
Comstock/Thinkstock: page 21.
Creatas Images/Thinkstock: page 163.
Hasnain Dattu: pages 48 and 71.
Yvonne Duivenvoorden: pages 14, 27, 28, 40, 51, 62, 76, 107, 117, 130, 164, 177, 184, 190, 196, 210, 213, 228 and 236.
Geoff George: page 5.
Edward Pond: pages 33, 39, 84, 93, 123, 154, 157, 158, 178, 189, 203, 221 and 245.
Jodi Pudge: pages 126 and 170.

David Scott: pages 54, 61, 69, 72, 87, 96, 148, 151, 183, 216 and 224.
Thinkstock: pages 57, 91, 141 and 173.
Andreas Trauttmansdorff: pages 17, 102, 120, 195 and 253.
Felix Wedgwood: pages 13, 34, 47, 83, 113, 114, 143, 147, 204, 209, 231, 254, 259, 262, 269, 274 and 279.

Food styling

Julie Aldis: pages 62 and 246.
Donna Bartolini: pages 48 and 71.
Andrew Chase: page 245.
Carol Dudar: page 138.
Ian Muggridge: page 170.
Lucie Richard: pages 13, 33, 34, 39, 40, 47, 51, 54, 61, 69, 72, 76, 83, 93, 96, 113, 114, 123, 143, 147, 151, 189, 204, 209, 216, 224, 231, 254, 259, 262, 269, 274 and 279.
Claire Stancer: pages 196, 203 and 228.
Claire Stubbs: pages 14, 17, 84, 102, 107, 117, 120, 126, 130, 154, 157,

158, 164, 177, 178, 183, 195, 210, 221, 236 and 253.
Rosemarie Superville: pages 28, 87 and 213.
Sandra Watson: page 184.
Marianne Wren: pages 27 and 190.
Nicole Young: page 148.

Prop styling

Laura Branson: pages 13, 33, 34, 47, 72, 83, 93, 113, 114, 123, 143, 147, 170, 189, 204, 209, 216, 224, 231, 254, 259, 262, 269, 274 and 279.
Catherine Doherty: pages 17, 27, 28, 102, 107, 120, 190, 195, 213 and 253.
Marc-Philippe Gagné: pages 164 and 177.
Maggi Jones: pages 138 and 151.
Chareen Parsons: page 246.
Oksana Slavutych: pages 14, 40, 48, 51, 54, 61, 62, 69, 71, 76, 84, 87, 96, 117, 126, 130, 148, 154, 157, 158, 183, 184, 196, 203, 210, 221, 228 and 236.
Genevieve Wiseman: page 178.